Peaker *of the* Peak

Letters to the Editor
2003–2022
18 Years of Observing
Hong Kong

MARK PEAKER

UNICORN

FOREWORD

For as long as I can remember reading the *South China Morning Post* in Hong Kong, there was one man writing regular letters to the editor, signed: *"Mark Peaker, The Peak"*.

It wasn't just the catchy signature that caught my eye back then; the letters were worth reading, providing a citizen's commentary on just about anything and everything – from mundane matters that might bother the man on the street to major issues transforming people's lives in this city.

It's the beginning of the year 2022 now, and Mark is still writing letters to the editor. And I daresay he's even more of a menace in this digital age, no longer fettered by the old inconvenience of having to mail physical dispatches from his home on The Peak.

Going through all his letters again now, neatly archived for everyone's reading convenience in this book, I'm struck by how they form a historical narrative and a chronicle of life in Hong Kong. And Mark's personal perspective offers a certain insight that you won't get from journalistic or academic accounts.

I never imagined, all those years ago, that I would be writing the foreword to this prolific letter writer's first book showcasing the very correspondence that caught my eye back then.

What a pleasure to present his work to readers again in its new avatar.

Yonden Lhatoo
Chief News Editor
South China Morning Post

INTRODUCTION

epistolary
adjective
UK /ɪˈpɪstəl.ər.i/
US /ɪˈpɪs.təl.er.i/

formal
involving or consisting of letter writing:
She wrote an epistolary novel.
They had an epistolary relationship.

The letters you are about to read are my epistolary relationship with the *South China Morning Post*, an affair which began in 2003 and continues to this day. I will admit I have not been entirely faithful, having had the odd letter published in the *Financial Times*, *The Telegraph*, *The Times*, *AutoCar* and *Country Life*. It is, however, my eighteen-year epistolary relationship with the *South China Morning Post* that has allowed this snapshot of modern Hong Kong history to be formed.

There is sadness, mounting anger and frustration, happiness and laughter. Some of it is mordant, some of it absurd, all of it a reaction to living in these extraordinary times that have shaped Hong Kong. My letters opine on diverse topics, capturing the capriciousness of our urban existence, often written whimsically but always with a view to create awareness – from government to politicians, taxi drivers to airlines, celebrities to royalty.

Hong Kong is an astonishing city. It is my home, and my observations over eighteen years of writing reflects an awareness of the pain, aspirations, joy and, at times, shame of our city. Hong Kong has changed since my first solitary letter in 2003 to my numerous letters in the latter years, a reflection of my commitment to continue to voice out my concerns, criticism or praise.

It is my expression of the recognisable aspects of life in Hong Kong.

Mark Peaker, The Peak

2003

Singapore leadership

Quite how Singapore Deputy Prime Minister Lee Hsien Loong can keep a straight face when stating governance of Singapore is not a family business amazes me ("Singapore deputy PM won't have a problem telling his father when to quit", October 13).

Perhaps looking up the word "nepotism" might be in order.

Mark Peaker,
Southern District

2004

Canopy vs Dome

I refer to the letter from R. E. J. Bunker (November 26) in which he compares the failed London Dome to the proposed development of West Kowloon Cultural District.

Mr Bunker misses two vital elements in his dismissal of the Hong Kong project. It is not located in the outskirts of the east end of London. And Hong Kong people will take this development to their hearts.

Whereas Londoners had no interest in travelling across the metropolis on wet miserable days on unreliable transport, Hong Kong people will flock to this stunning vision that will show this city to the world as truly international and inspirational.

Mark Peaker,
Chung Hom Kok

2005

Don't complain

I agree with the letter "Spoiled Hongkongers" (January 1).

This is not the time to criticise any government, charity, person or effort. The only people who should have a voice are those who perished. Their silence is deafening the entire world, and those who wish to criticise might do well to listen. To all those who are helping in any way and at any pace – thank you.

Mark Peaker, Chung Hom Kok

Mocking monarchy

Recalling the concern created last year by a shop's Nazi theme, I was appalled that Prince Harry donned a Nazi uniform at a party in England. This boy has made a mockery of all who support the institution of the monarchy and has shamed the honour of the dead.

Mark Peaker, Chung Hom Kok

Dynamic Hong Kong

I refer to Adrianne and Christopher Rush's letter headlined "Hong Kong declining" (February 18).

What complete rubbish! Hong Kong remains one of Asia's most dynamic cities. Hong Kong people retain their vitality for getting things done. Hong Kong's transport system remains the envy of virtually any world-class city. Its skyline is dominated by some of the world's most impressive buildings. Hong Kong's political relationship with the mainland is far from being "stymied", and "insignificant" news from the mainland is actually very relevant for a city that is a part of China!

Hong Kong will continue to go from strength to strength, that is the nature of its people, to move forward. Adversity, arguments, pollution, disaster – Hong Kong weathers all storms and survives. For those of us who live here, we are proud to be part of Hong Kong.

Mark Peaker, Chung Hom Kok

Hypocrisy over Pope

Oh, the hypocrisy of President George W. Bush and Secretary of State Condoleezza Rice kneeling in prayer before the body of Pope John Paul II. How dare these people, who have

brought death and misery to millions, and have, in the Pope's own words, caused a "clash of civilisations" kneel in prayer before a man opposed to everything they represent.

Mark Peaker, Chung Hom Kok

At Pope's funeral

In reply to the letter "Misplaced criticism" (April 11), by Stephen Anderson, Zimbabwe's Robert Mugabe is indeed beneath contempt, but he did not kneel in silent prayer before the body of Pope John Paul II. Further, I made no anti-American reference and it is puerile to suggest that I did. As for arresting other leaders, is it not further American hypocrisy that those states which kill innocents, flout UN resolutions and taunt the west, but have no oil to plunder, are free to do as they please?

Mark Peaker, Chung Hom Kok

Plumed chief

Should Donald Tsang Yam-kuen take up residence in Government House, he will have finally fulfilled his dream of becoming governor. If governor David Wilson left behind his plumage, all it will need is a little dusting off.

Mark Peaker, Chung Hom Kok

Condemn the IRA

Londoners know the sound of bombs, the nervousness one felt when a discarded paper bag was left on a seat next to you on the Tube. The Irish Republican Army campaigns made us all aware of terrorism long before 9/11.

Where was the American network coverage of the Harrods bombing, the Brighton bombing or the Docklands one? Of course then it was merely Britain's plight and the IRA drew huge financial support from the US. When Secretary of State Condoleezza Rice speaks of the need for a united front against terrorism, but fails to condemn the still active IRA, it insults the resolve of Londoners, who are sick of bombs but sick of lies, too.

Mark Peaker, Chung Hom Kok

Cull feral dogs

The culling of feral dogs at Disneyland should be commended. As a dog owner, I support all means to rid Hong Kong of the feral packs that roam the country parks and pose potential risks. While the killing of animals is regrettable, the problem is created by uneducated humans who adopt puppies, then dump them once the novelty has worn off. Goofy may be adorable, a disease-ridden feral dog biting your child is not.

Mark Peaker, Chung Hom Kok

Red, white and blue

Would someone tell Stephen Bradley, British consul general, that the Union Jack is not a piece of clothing to adorn his neck ("Help within hours for Britons caught in regional disasters", 8 August).

Mark Peaker, Chung Hom Kok

2006

No armchair analysis

I refer to the letter from Kwan Kai-man, "Struggle for some gays" (March 10).

He mentions: "… practised an active homosexual lifestyle for some time, but that lifestyle cannot satisfy their real selves".

Is this reader assuming that all that gay [men] do is engage in sexual activity as a means of trying to define who they are, and that to be "liberated from that inclination" is the only chance for peace of mind? Sexual awareness is part of defining all people, gay or straight. Is he advocating that we all liberate ourselves from these inclinations, or just gay people?

The struggle by gay people for acceptance is a struggle fought in the face of puerile and prejudiced comments, such as your reader demonstrates. The gay community is indeed diverse. Each day we all walk, work, talk and drink with its members, be they openly gay or not: your taxi driver, your teacher, your colleague, your best friend, your lawyer, and so on.

These people live with integrity and pride. They do not define themselves through their sexual exploits; rather, they share their lives with friends, family and partners, and contribute to society at all levels. The gay community does not require armchair analysis any more than it seeks pity or prejudice.

Mark Peaker, The Peak

Armchair judges unfair

Mount Everest is a killer and all who take her on realise this. To condemn double-amputee Mark Inglis from the comfort of one's armchair is profoundly unfair ("Descent into savagery", May 27). Only those climbing knew what was happening. I am sure the decision to leave David Sharp was not one Mr Inglis rushed into, nor one Sharp wished him to have to make. Sharp died embracing life, and it is not for anyone other than his family and Mr Inglis to ponder.

Mark Peaker,
The Peak

Elevated carbuncles

Should anyone have any doubts about the architectural merit of the Central Harbourfront project, then sadly their fears are confirmed by the hideous blue metal walkway that winds its way beside IFC [International Finance Centre].

Such prefabricated, elevated walkways already hang drearily over other streets in Hong Kong, doing nothing to enhance their environment. It is a travesty in the making. Of course, I am sure links to the ceremonial palace to be built at Tamar will be suitably grandiose.

Mark Peaker, The Peak

Choice of role model apt

How apt that our chief executive should hold Singapore's mockery of a democratic government up as a beacon of progress ("Tsang looks to Singapore for ideas", July 17). Quite where he intends to find a military to recruit political talent from in Hong Kong is interesting. As for recruiting a new layer of political appointees from the business community, isn't nepotism already alive and well and influencing policy in Hong Kong?

Mark Peaker, The Peak

Bush's baby talk vulgar

President George W. Bush has vetoed the US Congress' bid to lift funding restrictions on human embryonic stem-cell research ("Bush set for his first veto with stem-cell bill", July 20), ignoring the potential that it offers in treating Alzheimer's disease, Parkinson's, diabetes, spinal cord injuries and numerous other conditions.

On a carefully orchestrated stage filled with babies cooing and crying behind him, he argued that the bill "would support the taking of innocent human life in the hope of finding medical benefits for others". He said it crossed "a moral boundary that our decent society needs to respect". Each child on the stage, he said, "began his or her life as a frozen embryo that was created for in-vitro fertilization … These boys and girls are not spare parts".

How vulgar that he cries foul on this much-needed research and dares to cite moral boundaries when thousands of children die daily as a result of his administration's needless wars.

Perhaps his view is to breed them now, kill them later.

Mark Peaker, The Peak

Poor Princess Aiko

So, Japan has its male heir, and the future of the Chrysanthemum Throne is secure for the next generation. How bewildering that Japanese newspapers are already writing about the newborn prince's need to ensure his future wife also produces sons.

Of course, this argument is deeply rooted in Japanese culture, but one cannot help but feel pity for Princess Aiko, who is now relegated to the lower ranks and destined by imperial law to be expelled from the royal family on the day she marries.

Mark Peaker, The Peak

Ruling reflects reality

Alice Yeung misses the point in her letter criticising the Appeal Court's gay-sex ruling ("Setback for HIV battle", September 23).

First, she shows her ignorance of the fact that most people newly infected with HIV around the world are straight rather than gay. She further misses the point that the aim of the judgement is to have an age of consent that reflects the sexual activity of people.

Her belief that delaying the age of consent will delay sexual activity is perhaps based on her ignorance of sexual behaviour and the fact that aligning the age of consent allows young gay men to take full responsibility for their behaviour without being condemned as criminals. This more realistic approach to the behaviour of sexually active people, be they gay or not, is one of the best methods for teaching safe sex practices.

Mark Peaker, The Peak

North Korea's nuclear test an indictment of the world

How interesting that a country that posed no threat, had no nuclear capability or weapons of mass destruction is destroyed by invading American forces instructed by a president who ignores UN Security Council advice and whose actions have done nothing but escalate the global "war on terror". Yet, a country that flaunts its nuclear ambitions, mocks the western world and poses a real threat to our regional stability is able to carry out its first nuclear test. The demand of US President George W. Bush for an immediate response by the UN Security Council is deplorable and shows his war in Iraq was his personal agenda whilst the real threats to global stability are allowed to strengthen. Let's hope the more mature leaderships of Asia can bring the rogue state of North Korea back from the brink.

Mark Peaker, The Peak

Let them have buses

Forget the purchase of VW Phaetons and their petrol-guzzling engines. What our top officials need is a fleet of minibuses. We could even come up with an appropriate roof colour. These will ferry our hard-working senior bureaucrats from place to place with the added benefit of sparing the occupants the guilt they must surely currently feel being ferried at speed up empty bus lanes in their AM-registered 7-series BMWs while the rest of us sit gridlocked.

Mark Peaker, The Peak

Words of ignorance

I was initially unsure whether to reply to Chris Burdon's letter, "Learn the language" (November 5), in French, Basque or Catalan. How can a person who has lived in Hong Kong NOT know if Mandarin or Cantonese is the local language? This is indeed puzzling. His comment about "locals" – and by this I deduce he refers to taxi drivers, stallholders and other members of Hong Kong society who do not speak English – is equally puzzling and insulting. From wet markets to bakeries, the ability of local residents to speak English in order to accommodate us is there. Of course, there are times when the language barrier appears and at times it is frustrating, but it must be more frustrating for a Chinese person living in a city in China to be forced to speak English to a foreigner who has made no attempt to learn the local language. As for Mr Burdon's closing comment that it's worth learning Chinese to avoid being overcharged as a foreigner, perhaps he should take a closer look at the country he writes from – France, where everyone is ripped off, regardless of whether they speak French, Putonghua or English.

Mark Peaker, The Peak

None so blind as the man who will not see this filth

In her 1988 book *Hong Kong*, Jan Morris describes Victoria Peak, the island's highest point, as a place where "the hills of Guangdong stand blue in the distance ... you see the city itself precipitously below you. The early sun catches the windows of Kowloon across the water."

Perhaps we can invite Morris back to stand in the same spot now. I fear her words may read: "The hills of Guangdong stand hidden in a blanket of smog ... once there was a city itself shining precipitously below you. The early sun no longer catches the windows of Kowloon across a waterway that shimmers vainly under a grey opaque sky."

From my terrace on The Peak, I so rarely see those magnificent mountains that, when they do pop through the haze, I actually stop to look at them before they disappear again – blanketed in both pollution and ignorance from a chief executive who simply refuses to see what everyone else cannot see!

Mark Peaker, The Peak

2007

A majestic gesture

How nice that Prince Charles has decided to cancel his annual
skiing trip to reduce his carbon footprint ("Prince cancels ski
trip", January 21). No doubt this is entirely unrelated to the
fact that this is an appalling ski season and there is presently
no decent snow to ski on.

Mark Peaker, The Peak

A vote loser

Thursday night's election debate would have stirred many
offices debates the next day on the subject of universal
suffrage in Hong Kong. It certainly did in my office, where my
colleague asked why Hong Kong, given its "immense size",
should not have this right?

I am not convinced that Hong Kong, which benefits
enormously from its unique role with China, is correct to
pursue this course. Hong Kong must remember that it is a city
within China and, to correct my colleague's point of view, not
even a large city. With a population of some 7 million, Hong

Kong falls around 25th in the list of major Chinese cities (and their administrative regions).

Are Guangzhou, Tianjin, Xian, Harbin or Chengdu seeking universal suffrage? Hong Kong has a right to its identity and continued success but, as the British realised, Hong Kong without Beijing does not function, and I for one do not want border control restrictions every time I want to visit Kowloon!

Mark Peaker, The Peak

Ultimate price is cheapened

"They shall grow not old, as we who are left grow old. Age shall not weary them, nor the years condemn. At the going down of the sun and in the morning, we shall remember them, lest we forget."

Those are pertinent words for the memories of servicemen who paid the ultimate price. Now, the price is merely a payment for having been imprisoned and scared for a week or so. (Or it was, until the British defence ministry ruled against selling stories to the media by the 15 sailors and marines released by Iran.)

Where is the payment for the thousands of soldiers who die in active combat but are never thought "newsworthy"? These 15 were ready to bring shame on their regiments and disgrace to the memory of all those who fought and died before them.

Mark Peaker, The Peak

Paying the price for being late

Eugene Li, ("Hidden cost of budget airlines", April 23), seems to feel that those who pay budget airfares should not complain when they arrive late.

Perhaps he may want to explain why hundreds of people paying full first-class fares, business-class fares, economy-class and discounted economy are still arriving late on full-fare airlines that apparently have planes to spare? Except, of course, when one gets a technical hitch that strands passengers in London because there is no spare plane available. Having paid HK$70,000 for this inconvenience recently, I would be much happier being late for HK$16,000!

Mark Peaker, The Peak

Aids doesn't care whether you are gay or straight, black or white

I am writing in response to Peter Wei's veiled homophobic letter ("Homosexuals must face up to reality", June 10), as well as other recent ignorant letters. HIV/Aids is a chronic disease that affects more than just the small, mostly very aware, Hong Kong gay community.

It is this view that people like to believe: HIV infection only happens to gay people, sex workers and "people who sleep around". Many people think that if you are not gay, or a sex worker, you are "safe". This is not true. Types of sexual behaviour – not whether you are gay or straight, black or white – put you at risk of HIV infection.

South Africa has about 4.74 million people with HIV – and about 98 per cent of them are straight. Most do not know their HIV status because they have no access to medical centres that can carry out the required testing; this means that many people unknowingly pass HIV on to others.

Effective HIV prevention and treatment depends on people wanting to have an HIV test – and finding out if they are infected. But for as long as people continue to face discrimination, they will be afraid to volunteer for an HIV test.

Effective prevention and treatment also depend on people being more "open" about HIV and Aids. It depends on people not being afraid to tell their lovers, friends, family, and even colleagues. When people feel confident enough to come forward to tell others about their HIV status, ignorance and misunderstandings about HIV will start to break down.

Yes, the rise in the reported cases of HIV/Aids in Hong Kong is alarming, but it also means more people – gay and straight – are being tested.

What is required is a larger education programme to ensure safe sex practices are adhered to and to help end the ignorance of those who still feel HIV/Aids is a gay disease.

It is these people, such as Peter Wei, who need – to use his words – "to face up to reality and to think twice about their responsibilities to society and themselves".

Mark Peaker, The Peak

Can we have some clouds?

Now that the government has claimed responsibility and proclaimed itself the saviour of Hong Kong's recent record blue skies and cleaner air, could we perhaps ask them to billow in some white fluffy clouds in order to tone down the present soaring temperatures?

I am sure this is entirely within their new magical weather-making powers!

Mark Peaker, Central

Bank has long history in China

Hendrik-Jan Stalknecht said the Netherlands has no need for "that kind of money", when referring to the Singaporean and Chinese governments' interest in the takeover of ABN Amro Bank ("Dutch snub", August 1).

He might like to ponder the reality that ABN has been taking Chinese money for more than 100 years, having been established in Shanghai in 1903 and seemingly not feeling guilty for every guilder of profit made since then!

Mark Peaker, The Peak

Homosexuality does not lead to an unhappy life

I was aghast to read Gordon Truscott's letter that once again maligns gay people with the misconception that homosexuality leads to an unhappy life and ultimately HIV ("Help available for unhappy gays", August 16).

Mr Truscott is being hypocritical when he cites Exodus International as a bastion of moral righteousness and the saviour of homosexual souls.

He might want to point out, as he states "knowledge is power", that Exodus is a highly dubious US-based organisation that uses "reparative therapy" as a so-called "cure". It ignores the medical and scientific consensus that attempts to "eliminate" same-sex attractions are not effective and are potentially harmful.

The ethics and efficacy of these procedures are rejected by all mainstream medical and mental health associations that have taken a position on the topic.

Their stance is that sexual orientation is unchangeable, and that attempts to change that orientation is often damaging to the person's well-being.

The American Psychiatric Association states that "ethical practitioners refrain from attempts to change an individual's sexual orientation". Exodus claims to have "helped" hundreds of thousands of ex-gays and lesbians.

However, such a claim cannot be certified, as Exodus refuses to release any information on what that estimate is based on, or how the programme success rate is measured.

Perhaps Mr Truscott might also wish to explain why Exodus' first co-founding member, Michael Bussee, had to leave the group after he started a relationship with Gary Cooper – which resulted eventually in a life-commitment ceremony.

Rainbow works hard in Hong Kong to stop precisely the type of homophobic views expressed by Mr Truscott, and seeks to give counsel, friendship and comfort to people who find accepting their sexual orientation difficult. Mr Truscott is correct about one thing, however: his comment that "the realities of homosexuality are largely shielded from public view".

Yes Mr Truscott, the success, wealth, pride, ability and happiness of millions of gay people are shielded from the ignorance of people such as yourself.

Yet, they are shared openly with anyone who refrains from bigoted attacks that seek to destroy others.

Mark Peaker, The Peak

Airline doing a great job

There has been a lot of negative press about Cathay Pacific's Marco Polo redemption programme and the seemingly impossible task of booking flights.

I am here to praise the programme, the excellent assistance the staff give members and the lengths they go to in order to get passengers flights as close to the original itinerary as possible.

Yes, Cathay Pacific has a commercial responsibility and sells as many seats as it can.

However, if you plan in advance, are flexible with your dates and don't demand, for example, to fly on the eve of the Lunar New Year, then in my experience, Cathay will deliver on its redemption promise 90 per cent of the time.

Mark Peaker, The Peak

Airline still doing a great job

In response to S. Fournier's letter regarding Cathay Pacific's redemption programme ("Flier frustrated over Asia Miles", September 14), I am happy to inform him that I am a Diamond Marco Polo member. That reflects my loyalty to an airline that I think is the best in the air.

I was intrigued by S. Fournier's plight in booking flights to Bali, so I went online and checked for flights departing on October 1 and returning on November 1, the dates he mentioned.

The system immediately showed that I could redeem a return trip in business class for the dates, if not the class, cited by your correspondent.

As I mentioned in my letter ("Airline doing a great job", September 10), flexibility is the key to redeeming flights, and I again praise Cathay Pacific for offering an excellent reward programme.

Mark Peaker, The Peak

Lyrics for a smog-filled day

As Hong Kong chokes beneath our cloak of smog, I was bemused to see the 1970s pop group Air Supply was coming to Hong Kong.

Perhaps we should ask them to serenade our government with their song "Feel the Breeze" – its opening line slightly changed to say, "Since we elected you how can we but notice the sky once blue is now battleship grey, for here we stand outside choking into another polluted day."

Mark Peaker, The Peak

Stop Hong Kong's minibus maniacs

I am concerned about the number of accidents involving minibuses in Hong Kong. Is this the image Hong Kong wants? A collection of unruly, often unlicensed maniacs driving our friends, relations and children in a manner that totally disregards their safety?

When will the government act to compel all minibus drivers to take new, stringent driving tests and ensure that all minibuses are fitted with seat belts?

When will it limit the speed of minibuses, to stop them hurtling down narrow streets at excessive speeds?

How many people have to die before action is taken?

Mark Peaker, The Peak

Bad press for HK pollution

Attending an Islamic banking conference in Bahrain, I noticed a report in the *Bahrain Tribune* about pollution in Hong Kong.

It was embarrassing to have to try and defend the quality of life we know we should have in Hong Kong against comments condemning Hong Kong as "a filthy place to want to live or visit".

Given the conference is attended by some of the leading figures of Islamic financing, an area our hapless government seeks closer ties with, it is time for Chief Executive Donald Tsang Yam-kuen to do something to stop Hong Kong being condemned internationally as an unfit place to work.

Mark Peaker, The Peak

Bhutto tribute

This year ends with the senseless slaying of Benazir Bhutto, and Pakistan is plunged into an uncertain future that bodes badly for stability in the region and around the world.

Bhutto may have been tainted but she, like her father, believed in the future of a truly democratic Pakistan.

Her return to her beloved country may have been short, but her courage, her strength, her vision and her belief in the people of Pakistan will live forever. May her soul rest now in eternal peace.

Mark Peaker, The Peak

2008

Recycling law needed in HK

How distressing it is to read the claim that 500,000 television sets are to be dumped ("Green group fears mass dumping of old TV sets", December 31).

My brother visited Hong Kong over Christmas. Based in Switzerland, recycling to him is not only second nature, it is compulsory.

He was aghast at the waste he saw in Hong Kong and could not understand why a supposedly First World city has no recycling – a few small bins here and there are not the solution.

I sadly could not give him a satisfactory answer. Although I do separate my rubbish, once it passes from my home, I know it is all simply thrown together. It is time for the government to start placing large recycling bins in every area, and it must pass legislation forcing every residential development to have recycling bins either in each apartment or in the central refuse collection point. It must then ensure this separated refuse remains separated and recycled.

Hong Kong must step up to this challenge and cannot simply allow this "wrap it in plastic" mentality to continue.

Mark Peaker, The Peak

Cathay took note of critical views on seats

I write in response to Dick Groves' letter ("Cathay must think again about its new business class seats", January 15).

He comments that Cathay Pacific believes "in time, customers will adjust to the new product".

Initially, I was also not that impressed with the new Cathay Pacific business-class seat, feeling it was cramped and did not allow a passenger to look out of the window. Rather, it forces you to look at the feet of those opposite.

I raised these concerns with Cathay and they genuinely took my comments (and I am sure other passengers' comments) seriously. I can assure Mr Groves that Cathay (like any airline) is looking to refine its seats in line with passenger expectations. It is impossible to please every customer. However, having used the new seat a few times now, it is what most long-haul business-class customers want – flat and private.

The seats will see some modifications that are purely the result of Cathay Pacific listening to the comments of its customers.

Cathay Pacific remains something for Hong Kong to be proud of – a world-class airline for a world-class city.

Mark Peaker, The Peak

In defence of Hong Kong

So [outgoing British consul general] Stephen Bradley has told us that we are people with insufficient cultural taste and that one would find it difficult to say Hong Kong was a great city like New York or London ("'HK is falling short of greatness'", March 14). Is London's decrepit rail system better than Hong Kong's? Are London's exorbitant prices fairer than Hong Kong's? Is Manhattan as clean as Central? Do New Yorkers have an airport like Chek Lap Kok?

Culture is more than a roof over reclaimed land. Culture is derived from the passion of the people as reflected in our music and art.

Mark Peaker, The Peak

Honour at stake

On a day where global banks continued to write off billions of dollars but still reward their multimillion-dollar-salaried chief executives with severance packages that will ensure no mortgage concerns for them, I read that a family of three committed suicide for what appeared to be credit card debt ("Three die in family suicide over debts", April 2).

Perhaps this family felt shame and paid the ultimate price for their honour, which was far higher than that of the banks.

Mark Peaker, The Peak

Test bus drivers

The Hong Kong government should require all drivers of public vehicles to take stringent driving tests to safeguard the public.

The sight of grieving relatives after the bus crash in Sai Kung on May 1 was shocking. How many more accidents need to happen before the government acts?

Mark Peaker, The Peak

Worried over quake threat

Lam Chiu-ying, director of the Observatory, says the city's infrastructure – bridges, railways, tunnels and most buildings – can resist earthquakes with an intensity of VII (very strong) on the Modified Mercalli Scale.

However, he made absolutely no mention of the fact that a lot of Hong Kong is now built on reclaimed land.

In the Kobe earthquake that killed 6,279 people in 1995, districts built on reclaimed land suffered large-scale liquefaction – that is, some areas collapsed back into the sea.

What comfort can officials give us that such liquefaction will not happen here in Hong Kong?

Buildings may meet certain test requirements, but if the ground they are built on turns to liquid, what is the result – an IFC that drops from 88 floors to eight?

Mark Peaker, The Peak

Come out from JFK's shadow

So, Barack Obama has become the Democratic candidate and will now run against the veteran John McCain. Senator Obama is supposed to remind us of the halcyon days of the John F. Kennedy administration and its supposed glorious reign at a time when America was right and just. Kennedy served a mere 1,000 days in office before his tragic assassination ensured his martyrdom, and the myth of the Kennedys as America's "royalty" was cemented. Kennedy as president took us to the verge of nuclear war and his Bay of Pigs speech told of the demise of Cuba and other "soft societies".

Senator Obama may inherit the presidency of a country that has lost its standing in the international community, has lost respect from within and is perhaps the country most hated by the Muslim world, not without just cause.

He needs, therefore, to be more than the reincarnation of Kennedy. He needs to unite his divided party and country. He also must not follow the tired road map of the Israel/Palestine issue, but must secure for us all a lasting peace with Islam that will recognise the right of others to live with their religious beliefs and for America to further recognise the dominance of Asia. America remains for now the world's superpower, but plays its role like a child rattling a new toy.

With Senator Obama, we have a chance for America to mature and regain the trust of other nations that the Bush administration has squandered in pursuit of oil revenues and personal agendas.

Mark Peaker, The Peak

Games chaos on the cards

Attending an art auction in Shanghai, I was informed I could not bid as they didn't accept "foreign credit cards".

Raising the point that Hong Kong is not "foreign", but part of China, made no difference until the auction house owner arrived and informed his staff that Hong Kong was indeed part of China.

I hope someone has told Visa staff in Beijing this or the Olympics may have a few more hurdles than expected!

Mark Peaker, The Peak

A lot of hot air

Chief Executive Donald Tsang Yam-kuen said Hong Kong's heat is one of the challenges athletes will need to overcome in the Olympic equestrian events.

I assume gasping for air will also be part of the competition.

I am sure his people are proud of the fact that breathing is now an Olympic sport and the gold medal goes to our Legislative Council which does nothing but add to the hot air.

Mark Peaker, The Peak

Cathay right on carbon plan

Cathay Pacific's chief executive Tony Tyler paints an accurate picture when he describes the Europe-imposed carbon emission plan as nothing more than a revenue boost for European treasuries ("Europe carbon emission plan will cost airlines 'a fortune'", August 18). In fact, carbon offsetting is a highly controversial subject that highlights the very real difficulties in trying to follow an environmentally friendly lifestyle while enjoying the opportunities of modern existence.

Critics often point out that offsetting just encourages people to maintain their existing carbon-gluttonous lifestyles with a clean conscience.

Large-scale tree planting is fraught with difficulties. Some recent scientific studies indicate that tree planting in temperate regions has little effect on global warming (although there may be ecological and social benefits).

Carbon emission offsetting has to be more than a revenue earner and more than a conscience-cleansing exercise for those individuals and nations that offend the most.

Mr Tyler is correct to not want Cathay Pacific to be a part of this and to focus on real measures that ensure emission reductions benefit the planet and not the pocket.

Mark Peaker, The Peak

Little battlers

With global markets failing and everyone talking about the worst times since the 1930s, how refreshing to see HKR International planning a 64 per cent fare increase on its Discovery Bay ferry-run monopoly.

How welcome it is to see landlords trying to lock in 35 per cent rent increases on tenants renewing leases, and how delightful that – while thousands have lost all on their minibond investments – the staff of the company that originated them have had their record bonuses for 2008 and 2009 guaranteed.

It's a recession, Jim, but not as we know it.

Mark Peaker, The Peak

31/10/2008

Investors are responsible

DBS pledges compensation for minibond victims? Who is the victim here? Had the financial crisis not occurred and these minibond holders been making profits, would they not be rejoicing?

Would CITIC Pacific not be elated had the Australian dollar-euro foreign exchange deal locked in their A$450 million upside profit rather than dive into the abyss of unlimited loss? Risk is risk, and I believe the onus to understand what you are buying lies equally with the investor as it does with the seller.

Crying over spilt milk because the investment went sour is folly when the desire to make the investment was based on greed, not security. People need to realise that the art of money management is not simply to make money in a bull market – any fool can do that.

It is to preserve capital when markets fail by having understood risk and adhered to a basic rule of investing only in products the investor understands and the manager running the money understands.

Mark Peaker, The Peak

Dull decorations

Wandering around Hong Kong over the weekend I was struck by our soulless Christmas decorations. Where, I wondered, is Santa Claus? It seems the only recent "Ho ho ho" was the gay parade in Causeway Bay.

Come on Hong Kong, what's wrong with a fat bloke in a red suit wandering around wishing you a merry Christmas and giving out some Christmas hugs?

Mark Peaker,
The Peak

2009

20/01/2009

Gay community deserves better than a judgemental attitude

The letter from Michael Cheung ("Citybus entitled to refuse request", January 13) serves again to show the ignorance of those who assume to judge the gay community as the singular deliverers of HIV/Aids.

Using the refusal of Citybus "to allow one of its buses to be hired for a gay parade" as a platform to launch his ill-informed assault is laughable. Does he expect Citybus to ban gay passengers or fire its members of staff who are gay?

Perhaps he would like separate buses for gay passengers as apparently, according to him, the gay community is still to be defined by the government and the treatment yet to be revealed.

I wonder how close Mr Cheung knew these men who have left years of homosexuality to seek supposed happiness in marriage.

Those who seek to live behind the facade of marriage to appease the ignorance of family and friends often spend their lives in misery and, worst, deception. Being gay is not transient; it is from the womb to the tomb.

Mr Cheung further chooses to quote out of context to enhance his prophecy of doom the alarming figures raised by Tim

Brown. Dr Brown is a well-known supporter of various HIV/ Aids projects in China and a close adviser to the Advisory Council on Aids.

Mr Cheung should read the Legislative Council's "Panel on Health Services Prevention and Control of Human Immunodeficiency Virus (HIV)/Acquired Immune Deficiency Syndrome (Aids)" to better understand the significant steps the community has taken to ensure the figures that he quotes do not happen.

Mr Cheung ends his letter with the comment that "this will hurt everyone until a full discussion leads to a comprehensive plan of action".

Perhaps then he should stop rattling alarmist ideas and realise the work that various government and-non government agencies do in order to educate those exposed to HIV – straight and gay – of their need to be safe.

Education and acceptance are what is required Mr Cheung, not division and hate based on ignorance.

Mark Peaker, The Peak

15/02/2009

Count your blessings

For months we have listened to the woes of people bemoaning their fate as their investments have failed and they have "lost everything".

Perhaps these people should look into the eyes of the victims of Australia's tragic fires, for in their reflection they will see the true cost of having lost everything.

Mark Peaker, The Peak

Change sign

So, the American International Group does it again ("AIG likely to get US$30b in new bailout terms", March 2 and "AIG posts record loss of US$61.7b for quarter", March 3). Perhaps now it is time to change the massive sign atop AIG Tower in Central to IOU.

Mark Peaker, The Peak

Tragedy waiting to happen

Driving up Garden Road on Tuesday I encountered a traffic jam caused by three taxis incapable of continuing on the slightly wet roads as their rear tyres squealed, unable to grip the surface. Is this just another tragedy in the waiting? Clearly these cars' tyres are bald and unsafe, and yet nothing is done to enforce safety standards.

Do we have to wait until a taxi slides on wet roads into a group of innocent people before this government finally places the safety of its citizens ahead of the greed of those who run our public transport services?

Mark Peaker, The Peak

Support Cathay in difficult time

Cathay Pacific is hurting and it is part of the responsibility of Hong Kong people to support our local carrier as much as we can. Cathay cannot rely on government subsidies to offset losses and must compete in one of the most aggressively discounted airfare sectors in the world.

It is easy to see Cathay as just another part of the global meltdown. But when Oasis collapsed, who picked up its stranded passengers? When local charities need to send people to events, who is it that often donates their seats?

Cathay staff, from the board down, have been asked to take unpaid leave and forgo bonuses. Hong Kong travellers need to show that we too are proud to help and ensure an icon of Hong Kong survives.

Mark Peaker, The Peak

Anger justified

I read with disgust the article by Shaikh Azizur Rahman about the self-gratification of Kumari Mayawati ("A monumental blunder by India's 'Dalit Queen'", July 11).

You reported that Ms Mayawati faced a backlash from "Dalits or untouchables", because she had been "using public money to erect dozens of statues of her party's leaders, including six of herself".

One can only hope her vanity will switch from statues to fountains. Then, at least, her people might have a source of drinking water.

Mark Peaker, The Peak

Minibus shame

Finally, this government acts ("Speed limiters eyed for all minibuses by 2011", July 29).

It took another four lives of its citizens for the Transport Department to realise all the letters, complaints and warnings over the appalling safety issues surrounding minibuses were not without just cause.

The government can hang its head in shame with the realisation that the deaths of many of the victims of minibus accidents could have been avoided and it would have cost a mere HK$5,000 – the average price of the speed limiter. That is slightly less than the cost of the airbag fitted to the Passat the transport minister drives.

Mark Peaker, The Peak

Wrong location for restaurant

Surely the manager of Caviar Kaspia can see what others cannot see when he states that "customers may retreat when they see the sumptuous outlook of our restaurant" ("Diners choose chicken over caviar as downturn bites", August 3).

Perhaps he has had one spoon of beluga too many. Most people will not spend thousands of dollars to sit in the middle of what was a passageway in the Landmark with a view of nothing more than escalators and the faces of passers-by who peer mockingly as they scurry past.

Perhaps Caviar Kaspia should understand the difference between humility and pretension.

Mark Peaker, The Peak

Prime site's "green" potential

Hong Kong is a dense urban space that leaves little room to build except to "go up".

The proposed towers of Wharf Holdings and New World cannot be condemned before they are built, for these buildings are integral to the continued growth of Hong Kong as a viable commercial centre. However, what can be questioned, and The Masterpiece is an example of this, is the dull, unimaginative and non-green intrusive architecture that takes away more than it gives in return.

Wharf Holdings' prime site at Harbour City affords it the opportunity to build something that reflects Hong Kong's commitment to its commercial future as well as its environment. Skyscrapers can be part of the solution to environmental problems, rather than the source.

Wharf Holdings has an opportunity to place an emphasis on design approaches, including natural ventilation, daylight and vertical landscaping to reduce energy use and define the future of environmentally sound buildings for Hong Kong.

Mark Peaker, The Peak

Obama should tighten own belt

US President Barack Obama is clueless. He came to power promising "Yes we can" and has proved resoundly, "No he can't".

He is printing money, bending to pressure groups and ransoming the future of his country for the vanity of his sure-to-be one-term presidency.

For a man who preaches to Americans that they must rein in their own spending, he sees no fault in holidaying at Martha's Vineyard, or allowing his wife and children to frolic around Paris, all this being paid for by taxpayers.

A blowout of the national debt to more than US$12 trillion is a nail in the coffin of a global recovery, and this administration has broken its pledge, mortgaged its authority and bankrupted its morality.

Mark Peaker, The Peak

24/09/2009

Pledges have hollow ring

I refer to the letters by Paul Serfaty ("Blame Bush for the mess", September 15) and Reuben M. Tuck ("Obama cleaning up Bush's mess", September 17) replying to my letter on US President Barack Obama ("Obama should tighten own belt", September 11).

I don't recall saying Mr Obama was worse than George W. Bush as president. I stood aghast as we watched Mr Bush engage in a needless war with a country guilty of no crime save a dislike of America and its flawed values.

I have felt the financial fallout of eight years of Republican over-spending to continue the American dream as keenly as the next man. I have seen little of the change, stability and hope Mr Obama was elected to bring. Indeed, Mr Tuck is correct, as is Mr Serfaty, that Mr Obama has inherited a plethora of problems from perhaps the worst president to ever hold office.

As an Englishman, I am not a US voter, yet I, like many, watched keenly as then Senator Obama engaged the world in his election bid.

So, Mr Tuck, what has this to do with Hong Kong directly? Nothing at all, but as the world's supposed greatest democracy dillies and dallies, I believe we are all entitled to voice our opinions.

Mark Peaker, The Peak

Leave nature to its own devices

Perhaps the relevant government departments that desire to concrete over Hong Kong by walling up our beaches, cementing over our country trails or railing in our city walks should look at the recent collapse of an important rock formation on Australia's south coast.

Surely if these magnificent obelisks, the Three Sisters, were under Hong Kong jurisdiction they would have long ago been cemented in and the sea reclaimed.

However, in a refreshing and perhaps poignant reminder in these ecological friendly times, Australia's tourism minister ruled out any rescue efforts (of what were originally thought to be the Twelve Apostles formation), saying nature should be left to take its course – apt words indeed.

Mark Peaker, The Peak

Israel's wall imprisons hope

This week, the world celebrated the anniversary of the tearing down of the Berlin Wall, which divided a nation and its people.

How sad, then, that Israel continues to extend the 700-kilometre barrier that seeks to isolate and divide the peoples of that region and has been condemned by the International Court of Justice as "contrary to international law".

Have we as a people, and the Jews as a race, not learned that division will never heal wounds and this barrier does not keep evil out; it keeps hope imprisoned?

Mark Peaker, The Peak

Return our tree

Does the government have no heart? The Christmas tree in Central is an integral part of the mood of Hong Kong.

Chief Executive Donald Tsang Yam-kuen may have few reasons to be cheerful this season, but he shouldn't deny a little joy to the children who flock to see a huge tree adorned with lights. If Santa is not looking, Mr Tsang can get the lights supplied by a family member!

Come on, give us back our Christmas tree.

Mark Peaker, The Peak

2010

06/02/2010

The right flight

I recently travelled to France where I joined friends who flew from London, Australia, Malaysia and the US. I was not surprised to hear their collective tales of woe from their respective airlines.

Delays, crowded airports, surly attendants and old planes were all part of the conversation. Not so for those of us who flew from Hong Kong on Cathay Pacific and enjoyed superior service, as ever.

Mark Peaker, The Peak

05/04/2010

Think outside the retail box

How apt that the photo of the "first cultural walk staged by the Tourism Board" ("Trail-blazer", March 27) showed a retailer shopping.

When will the people at the tourism office realise that Hong Kong abounds in natural beauty, wildlife, remote islands, ancient history, local theatre and art?

Perhaps they think Hollywood Road is entertainment and "that's all folks".

Mark Peaker, The Peak

15/04/2010

Let Interpol probe abuse

Cardinal Angelo Sodano tells the Pope that, "Holy Father, on your side are the people of God, who do not allow themselves to be influenced by the petty gossip of the moment" ("Top cardinal defends Pope against 'petty gossip'", April 5).

The young boys who were sexually abused entrusted their moral and spiritual safety to the clergy who betrayed this trust then hid behind the power of the church. This is not "petty gossip", it is an active, well-orchestrated and shamelessly protected paedophile ring.

Such systematic abuse over decades requires a full international Interpol investigation with the complete co-operation of the church.

Bishops and priests who are found guilty should be stripped of their office and incarcerated like anyone else found guilty of such a crime. Should Pope Benedict be found to have been complicit [in failing to act against these priests], he must also step aside.

Mark Peaker, The Peak

Pointless Old Peak Road wall would block a lovely view

Most days, I will walk my three dogs down Old Peak Road, along Tregunter Path and back up Chatham Path, before returning home to Barker Road.

Last year, I observed in slight bewilderment the furious welding of metal grates over the existing concrete barriers that have quite suitably prevented babies, animals and I suppose some rather clumsy people from falling into them.

Of course, the Lands Department needs to spend our money, and I suppose some person who has probably never walked the leafy and magnificent paths that criss-cross Hong Kong thought it would be a great idea to cage in these offending and potentially life-threatening places.

A week last Sunday I was stopped at a particularly beautiful part of Old Peak Road. After it has rained you can observe a magnificent waterfall gently cascading down the rocks trying to find its way to a harbour that is getting farther and farther away.

A young lady was asking people to sign a petition to stop our government from building a wall at this very spot. This wall will block the view of the trees and the waterfall.

The government tells us it is to protect people from falling off.

I am curious. Since Old Peak Road was built, I wonder just how many people have fallen off?

My guess is no one, and even if they did, we are not exactly talking about Mount Everest here.

But yet again our beloved government seems intent on taking whatever is left of Hong Kong and pouring concrete over it, walling and railing it in, or reclaiming it, with no understanding that, left alone, these places will manage just fine.

About 30 people signed the lady's petition when I was there, and I hope she gets many more signatures. Then we can send a message to the government to stop walling us in and stop treating Hong Kong people like babies.

We can manage to stay on the right path – we promise not to fall off.

Mark Peaker, The Peak

14/05/2010

Britain should call fresh polls

As I watched the comings and goings of politicians and worryingly unelected advisers jockeying with each other for the tenancy of Number 10, I was struck by the reality that the new British government was being formed behind closed doors with a party that garnered only 23 per cent of the popular vote – yet its leader is now deputy prime minister.

Nick Clegg offered himself to the two main parties in their search for power, and it was finally Conservative leader David Cameron who found himself in bed with the Liberal Democrats.

Mr Cameron has secured his Commons majority but at what price, and how long can this hastily arranged marriage last? This is not the government Mr Cameron desired nor the electorate voted for; Mr Clegg's party, let us remember, was not thought by [most] voters to be worthy of representation in Westminster. It saw its seats reduced and yet now finds itself with five cabinet places.

Mr Clegg certainly won the horse trading, forcing Mr Cameron into a coalition that has shaken democracy, traumatised the backbenches and left the people bereft of the government they wanted. How long can this last? Let the people choose again, go back to the polls and perhaps we might see a majority government elected by the people, for the people.

Mark Peaker, The Peak

Exits, stage left

I could not help but notice Rolex's Wimbledon promotion featuring Serena Williams and informing us: "From a country that gave us Shakespeare, surely we wouldn't expect our tennis matches to be any less dramatic."

Having watched the woeful performances of most of the women's draw, the Bard's words are indeed apt. However, methinks he would have called it "A comedy of errors".

Mark Peaker,
The Peak

Gays deserve fairer workplace

Chan Yuen-wang's call for fairer treatment of homosexuals and legislation against discrimination on the basis of sexual orientation is a brave declaration which deserves respect ("One march, a cross-section of social causes", July 2).

However, it is not just the government that needs to adopt a fairer attitude to the lesbian, gay, bisexual and transgender (LGBT) community. Corporations must also implement a fairer and more inclusive workplace for these employees. This was recently acknowledged with the publication of "Creating Inclusive Workplaces for LGBT Employees" sponsored by Goldman Sachs and IBM. As an openly gay businessman, I have personally been on the receiving end of office homophobia.

An example of this happened to me while working for a German bank. I was astounded as a senior manager came running into the dealing room, telling everyone at the top of his voice that I was gay.

My colleagues did know, yet the embarrassment I felt was not diminished by my own ease with my sexual orientation or the support given to me by my colleagues, who were more enraged than I over the incident.

The need for openness in the workplace may be an odd concept; do I reveal my sexuality or do I allow my work itself to define my success? Why do I, as a gay person, feel the need to open myself fully to others when I do not seek the same level of divulgence? "Creating Inclusive Workplaces for LGBT Employees" is a positive step. It is one the government should follow, ensuring Chan Yuen-wang's call for fairer treatment of homosexuals and enabling all minority groups to work free from harassment and ridicule.

Mark Peaker, The Peak

Part of city's rich fabric

David Tang Wing-cheung is quite correct in his defence of Cantonese ("Offensive views on Cantonese condescending", August 10).

The language is a core thread that embroiders the rich fabric of the life of Hong Kong.

Far from forgetting the language, all *gweilos* should be made to learn it, preventing many temper tantrums by frustrated foreigners whose own linguistic limitations are forever in the shadow of multilingual Hong Kong.

Mark Peaker, The Peak

Appalled by attack on tree

Sitting on my Peak balcony overlooking Hong Kong Island, I was sheltered by a lovely tree that has happily reached to the skies for over a decade.

That was until last Monday, when my neighbour's contractor decided to fell half of it so his boss could have a better view.

In my outrage, I demanded a stop to the axe-wielding by a totally inexperienced worker who was hacking away at this beautiful tree. The worker thought it was just a joke until I called the police, who responded immediately and the smiles soon ceased.

The government needs to remind all workers that trees are protected and cannot just be cut down to suit someone's whims. A tree is a life. Remove the skin of the earth and disaster follows.

Mark Peaker, The Peak

Cathay went the extra mile

With the recent rhetoric about Cathay seats, I thought I would write to remind people of just how good Cathay Pacific are.

A friend of mine sadly passed away in Taiwan and the efforts of the Cathay team in Taiwan in assisting with the local authorities were of immense help. Cathay staff went out of their way to ensure numerous parties coordinated their responsibilities. Cathay liaised where asked and took the initiative to ensure other requirements were met ahead of time. Cathay proved they are more than a seat.

Mark Peaker, The Peak

Overwhelming opposition

The continued persistence of the Lands Department to defy the will of the people, in its ridiculous plans to erect concrete walls at several points along Old Peak Road, must cease.

There is no requirement for these walls, and the department's attempts to waste public money and enrage the community with yet more needless destruction of Hong Kong's diminishing natural beauty is beyond reproach.

There is clear opposition to the building of these walls, and officials should listen to the people who use the trails.

How many more petitions, complaints or requests does the chief executive need before he hears the voices of the people of Hong Kong?

Mark Peaker, The Peak

2011

HK children suffer in silence

The declining quality of air in Hong Kong continues to add to our city's diminishing allure as a destination for tourists and relocating executives.

However, both these groups have a choice: they can visit or move to any number of destinations that offer cleaner air.

Reports of expatriate children fleeing with their parents barely a year after arriving is less of a cause for concern than the thousands of Hong Kong children who silently suffer the same symptoms but have no option but to endure.

Our government ought to explain its continued lack of policy on clean air to them; perhaps an annual State of the Health of Our Children address might finally allow this government to understand the reality that Hong Kong air is killing us.

Mark Peaker, The Peak

Too many jobs at arts hub

The West Kowloon Cultural District does not need another head count. Immersing this already submerged project with yet more administration is ridiculous.

Lee Wing-tat is correct to question the validity of needing a deputy chief executive officer ("Next arts hub chief may get a deputy to share workload", January 15). Perhaps we should also ask why on the Cultural District website the following positions have been advertised since 2009 – chief executive officer, senior executive assistant to the CEO, executive assistant to the CEO, personal secretary to the CEO, and director, CEO's office.

Presently there are more than 60 vacant positions, most a year past their closing date.

Perhaps the website is just outdated and they need a secretary to assist the assistant to assist the executive who can inform the senior executive to inform the secretary to the CEO to inform the executive assistant to the CEO to inform the senior executive to the CEO to inform the CEO, who, of course, does not exist.

Mark Peaker, The Peak

Ironic loss

I refer to the report about Stanley Ho Hung-sun ("How the elderly tycoon found out he was poor, and what he did about it", January 27).

When he found out that his personal fortune was worth a mere HK$600, it made me think that is probably how many of the patrons of his casinos feel most days.

Mark Peaker, The Peak

Find source of harbour E. coli

Escherichia coli bacteria is an elegant description for the massive increases in the excrement now floating in our waters ("Dirtier harbour defies logic with treatment in place, expert says", February 12).

It is simply not acceptable that those charged with ensuring the quality of water in our harbour are "frustrated".

Somewhere, tonnes of untreated excrement is pouring into our harbour and endangering us all.

Stop theorising about what may have gone wrong and find the source of this problem before our beaches become dunes of excrement and our harbour truly fragrant.

Mark Peaker, The Peak

Christchurch tragedy

The tragedy that has torn Christchurch apart is heart-wrenching.

However, it should remind us that Hong Kong is not immune to seismic activity and that many buildings here were constructed on reclaimed land.

Christchurch has shown that buildings in a country with world-class building codes for earthquake-proof structures can fall. One wonders how Hong Kong's skyscrapers would cope. The measures our government has in place must be made public.

Mark Peaker, The Peak

Wild dogs cull long overdue

Toh Zheng Han has every right to be angry after being bitten by "two large black dogs" ("Dogs a danger to the public", March 25).

However, he does not clarify if these were domesticated or wild feral dogs.

Hong Kong has a growing and out of control wild dog problem. These animals roam in packs, scavenge for food, breed uncontrollably and are indeed a danger to the public.

As the owner of three domesticated dogs, I agree with Mr Toh completely and request the government to start a cull of wild dogs to prevent further attacks.

Mark Peaker, The Peak

Wild dogs pose a real threat to HK people

Bernard Lo's love of all beings is commendable ("Live and let live with city's 'stray' cows", April 17).

Indeed, the birds that flit around our skies are strays, free to fly wherever the winds carry them.

However, I am much happier to be the target of bird droppings than I am to have my hand badly bitten by a wild dog. So, unless Alfred Hitchcock's classic film *The Birds* becomes reality, let's focus on the very real danger wild dogs pose to the safety of Hong Kong people.

Mark Peaker, The Peak

US was wrong to kill bin Laden

The atrocities that took place on September 11, 2001, were barbaric acts carried out by cowards who sought to kill innocent people in the name of their chosen god.

Yet to call the subsequent murder of Osama bin Laden justice is equally barbaric.

Murder can never be called justice, unless that sentence is passed down by a court of law, in this case the war crimes tribunal based in The Hague. That bin Laden was a murderer was never in dispute.

However, his assassination has not only given fuel to his followers, it has deprived the world of the opportunity to interrogate the leader of al-Qaeda.

We could have evaluated how he could have evaded global efforts to locate him for over a decade and truly gained an insight into the workings of the world's leading terrorist organisation.

The rash decision to execute this man was the wrong choice, for now the United States has unleashed the wrath of tyranny when it had a true opportunity to destroy terrorism from within.

Mark Peaker, The Peak

14/05/2011

US had no right to deny justice

I refer to the letter by Keith McNab ("Bin Laden trial a naive idea", May 7).

It is indeed naive to suppose justice would be administered by the US, which is incapable of upholding international values, preferring to set its own rules and be answerable to no one. Osama bin Laden, an unarmed person, had implied, not proven, links to the 9/11 atrocities, but that was for the US enough evidence to execute a man who may, however unlikely, have been innocent. That is why we have international laws – to contain rogue individuals and rogue countries.

Bin Laden was not the property of the US government to hunt down and kill. The tragedy that was 9/11 killed not only Americans; it was an international death toll, and the perpetrator should properly be brought before an international court to be answerable to the citizens of all countries who lost loved ones.

The US had no right to deny justice nor to be judge, jury and executioner.

Mark Peaker, The Peak

Li not best choice for role model

How predictable that Chief Secretary Henry Tang Ying-yen holds Li Ka-shing up as the example Hong Kong people should try to emulate ("Tang in no rush to take the top job", May 23).

Proof once again that this administration lives in awe of and remains subservient to the tycoons who run our city. Could our chief secretary and front runner for chief executive not have cited our city's world-class surgeons or leading scientists or sportspeople as those to follow, or is wealth the only measure of success our government can understand?

Hong Kong is prosperous because of the fabric of its people, not the cost of cloth on a rich man's back.

Mark Peaker, The Peak

Mothers ignore road traffic rules

Susannah Hirst correctly comments on the availability of exclusive parking offered only to Hong Kong's elite ("Tai-tais and bosses must be stopped from causing such serious congestion", June 1).

This abuse of the traffic law is, however, not purely a *tai-tai* creation; try driving along Stubbs Road at Bradbury School, during the pick-up and drop-off hour. Mothers seem to think it their divine right to mount kerbs, make illegal U-turns and double-park with absolutely no concern for the obstruction they cause. Membership of the double yellow line club is a privilege indeed.

Mark Peaker, The Peak

19/07/2011

Same-sex couples face biased policy

It is interesting that the Immigration Department now allows partners living in a same-sex relationship extended visa status, and it is curious that this is done on a case-by-case basis rather than accepting the reality of allowing same-sex partners equal rights across the board.

Civil partnership recognition is well established in a number of countries, and Hong Kong needs to recognise this status at all levels: from immigration to club membership.

The term spouse can no longer be defined as the wife of a man, and partners living in stable relationships must be allowed to live with their loved ones free of judgement from the authorities.

Hong Kong's immigration stance is a small step forward, but until a policy that accepts same-sex partnership as equal is made law, inequality and a need to be vetted every six months remains a biased government attitude.

Mark Peaker, The Peak

Interference on almost daily basis

One assumes John C. M. Lee lives in awe of the United States ("Don't meddle in America's own affairs", July 25).

How else can he explain his bizarre defence of the US when being criticised by China over President Barack Obama's meeting with the Dalai Lama?

As Mr Lee correctly observes, the US is a sovereign nation, as is China, yet this does not stop Washington making almost daily comments on how China should sort out its internal affairs, comments that are equally without merit and degrade relations far more than this one visit.

Mark Peaker, The Peak

Callous rich a cause of social unrest

The use of violence against property or persons cannot, of course, be condoned; however, such unrest is not without some just cause.

The great creation of wealth has given rise to an international society where the needs of the many are ignored at the behest of the few. Elected leaders respond to global chief executives rather than those who elected them.

Hong Kong should watch this worrying trend. Where absolute wealth sits uneasily beside a burgeoning working class, unrest will soon follow. At present, Hong Kong remains a civil and orderly society, yet it takes the smallest of incidents to trigger a chain reaction.

With snide comments from property tycoons, hospital queues that never end, and the bailing out of companies that find billions to buy their board members mansions in Shek O but cannot make a listed company profitable, eventually the people will react.

When even to remain poor requires a 50-hour work week, the milk will soon turn sour.

Mark Peaker, The Peak

25/08/2011

Put smoke detectors in all flats

The call for sprinkler systems to be installed in pet shops following the Happy Valley fire surely should prompt the requirement for smoke detectors to be installed in all residential apartments, in particular housing estates.

The lack of this requirement in densely populated tower blocks is absurd, and a disaster is just waiting to happen. Our government should of course pay the cost of installation, surely less than HK$6,000 per resident per apartment.

Mark Peaker, The Peak

12/09/2011

Landlubber laziness is to blame

Ken Wake's letter regarding the debris left in the wake of his recent boat trip ("Get tough with marine litter louts", September 8) is of interest in so much as the policing of our waterways with regard to dumping (from ships) is actually stringent.

The pollution that finds its way into our harbour comes mainly from land garbage washed down from streams, storm water outlets, levees and so forth, where there is little policing or control by the Food and Environmental Hygiene

Department. The problem is indeed not shipshape; it is
landlubber laziness.

Mark Peaker, The Peak

24/09/2011

Hong Kong has vibrant arts scene

I refer to the letter by Norman de Brackinghe on the arts in
Hong Kong ("Lively art scene is fragmented", September 20).
He talks about the difference between the treatment of the
arts in this city and in Seoul, and describes South Korea's
26th Asian International Art Exhibition, where 11 countries
participated.

Perhaps he failed to attend ArtHK11 [Hong Kong
International Art Fair] where a record number of
international and Asian artists exhibited their work for
the first time. Later this year, Fine Art Asia, a wholly Hong
Kong-created and -run event, will celebrate its seventh
year, bringing again a record number of local, Asian and
international artists to Hong Kong.

Mr de Brackinghe is not entirely wrong in his frustration with
Hong Kong's art scene. While the local Chinese media turns
out in force to openings, launches or artists' interviews, the
same cannot be said of the English-language media, which
rarely does.

As the co-founder and CEO of one of Hong Kong's largest art
spaces, I have witnessed the array and diversity of art that is
being brought to Hong Kong. It is growing, and appreciation
of this art is affecting all parts of society.

The West Kowloon cultural hub remains an enigma and it is
not yet clear what impact it will have on our arts scene in the
future.

We hope that in the years to come, the vast sums spent on the Cultural District will yield results and we will have a platform that can enhance an already vibrant arts scene.

The Arts Centre and the Academy for Performing Arts also play a significant role in educating Hong Kong's youth in all elements of art, and their continued work deserves praise.

Hong Kong has excellent curatorial ambassadors, and the recent surge in art activity, be it at the gallery or public display level, continues to define Hong Kong as a significant part of the Asian and international art market.

Mark Peaker, co-founder and CEO, 3812 Contemporary Art Projects

08/10/2011

Honesty still a politician's best policy

Henry Tang Ying-yen's admission of adultery was a brave move and leaves him open to the accusation that he timed his statement purely in pursuit of his desire to be chief executive, which is, of course, true ("'Unfaithful' Tang comes clean", October 5).

Yet, he has demonstrated strength of courage, and the remorse and guilt he feels towards his wife, Kwok Yu-chin, is real. He has shown an ability to be humble and to connect with the people of Hong Kong.

Honesty, no matter how contrite, remains a politician's best policy.

Mark Peaker, The Peak

Players are gay role models

Jan Olsen is correct that real men play rugby; real gay men that is ("Real men play rugby, not soccer", October 22).

Gareth Thomas from Wales and Ian Roberts from Australia are both openly gay international players whose decision to come out took courage; their bravery will have encouraged many young gay people struggling in the face of ridicule that homosexuality is part of the fabric of men from all walks of life.

Role models of this stature assure those coming to terms with their own sexuality that success in the face of ignorance can be achieved, [and that] being gay is to be a man.

Mark Peaker, The Peak

Money can be put to better use

The decision to formally declare Ho Tung Gardens a historic monument is folly. Our government needs to realise that a large house with a large garden is not necessarily relevant to the cultural heritage of Hong Kong, or to its people. Our truly historic buildings, those that were part of the foundation of Hong Kong, were long ago demolished to create the abyss of mediocrity that is Mid-Levels.

Preserving our heritage is important, but at what cost? HK$3 billion could be used to build a new children's hospital, or better care facilities for the elderly. It should not be used to preserve a building that, while it has an interesting history, will, after restoration and years of wrangling over what to use it for, sit empty and forgotten.

Mark Peaker, The Peak

Appalled by selfish drivers

Hong Kong is a city proud of its adherence to the law, making our metropolis a safe and secure place in which to live.

Our traffic police, however, fail to live up to this mark of excellence. I drive around Hong Kong each day and daily I witness a growing number of flagrant traffic offences. The most common and alarming is the running of red lights by buses. Yet perhaps the most disruptive remains the complete blockage of lanes outside the Landmark and IFC [International Finance Centre] buildings.

Three lanes are reduced to one, and at times none, while drivers await their masters who apparently are so important that we must all stop and anticipate their arrival.

I recently observed total blockage at IFC while across the road three police officers on motorcycles looked on and did absolutely nothing.

There is little point in building new roads to ease Hong Kong's traffic congestion when the police fail to enforce parking violations and roads become exclusive parking zones for Hong Kong's supposed elite.

Mark Peaker, The Peak

2012

11,000 would benefit from guide dogs

Underlying the story of the guide dogs Google and Iris ("Custody battle over guide dogs", December 24) is the frightening fact that since 1975 only two dogs have been brought to Hong Kong despite the fact there are 11,000 persons whose lives would be greatly enhanced with dogs as seeing-eye companions.

The regulations banning canines from most places are easily fixed: you merely add the phrase "except guide dogs".

Mark Peaker, The Peak

On wrong side of public opinion

Chief executive hopeful Henry Tang Ying-yen tells us "Not to worry" about the potential hazards of allowing mainland drivers in to Hong Kong.

It appears our former chief secretary, like those drivers from across the border, is clearly on the wrong side of public opinion and heading for a collision.

Mark Peaker, The Peak

Just build it, never mind the name

The West Kowloon Cultural District Authority cries that it may be in need of an extra HK$16.4 billion on top of the HK$21.6 billion already set aside ("Arts hub may cost taxpayers extra HK$16b", March 13).

It argues that bad investments have not yielded the returns required, and calls upon taxpayers to fund this incompetence. Is the cultural district a Greek bank, one wonders?

More than a decade of wrangling, manipulation and deception has left Hong Kong unable to achieve what the Basque government built in Bilbao, Spain, in a mere four years – one of the world's most iconic buildings, the Guggenheim Museum Bilbao.

It has established the city as an international destination for art and culture.

Michael Lynch, chief executive of the authority, now tells us that something that doesn't actually exist is in need of rebranding, mocking the custom of fung shui [sic] but happy to expend millions of our dollars to come up with a name for a development that will always simply be referred to as West Kowloon.

Hong Kong once had a reputation for getting things done, but seemingly now West Kowloon has become our own Greek tragedy.

Mark Peaker, The Peak

Bureau fails to preserve city's heritage

As another piece of Hong Kong's colonial architecture was needlessly demolished, one wonders if the motto of the Development Bureau's heritage website, "Conserve and revitalise Hong Kong heritage", can be taken seriously ("Old townhouses razed to clear site for apartments", March 27).

These magnificent houses, built as individual homes between 1925 and 1937, were all that remained of the once glorious Kennedy Terrace. Although they had been abandoned for more than a decade, there was always optimism these buildings would find a new purpose, optimism raised when banners that announced "Revitalising Hong Kong's Old Buildings" were draped over the scaffolding.

Sadly, these words were a facade, and the terraces were reduced to rubble.

The development secretary should explain why her bureau was so easily persuaded to allow the destruction of the very heritage she is tasked to preserve.

Mark Peaker, The Peak

Use cash for world-class facility

Jeffrey Lam Kin-fung, chairman of the assessment committee of the Mega Events Fund, seems eager to give away more of the HK$100 million the fund was allocated in the 2009 budget ("Mega Events Fund relaxes the rules", May 14).

Perhaps he may want to spend some of our millions buying a few hundred shovels as a gift to the West Kowloon Cultural District Authority, to allow it to start digging some foundations to build a cultural centre worthy of the international acts that bypass Hong Kong for other Asian cities that offer world-class facilities.

Mark Peaker, The Peak

Hong Kong is welcoming to gays

Jerome Yau makes some engaging comments on discrimination against gays ("Gays should have legal protection", May 23). However, as an openly gay person in Hong Kong, I differ with this insistence from the community that we all suffer acrimoniously at the hands of a hostile and prejudiced society.

Acceptance of the differences of all people regardless of faith, gender and sexual orientation is the goal of a tolerant society. Yet in supposedly more diversity-mature cities like Sydney, London or New York, the hostility shown towards lesbian, gay, bisexual and transgender (LGBT) people – as reflected in, for example, hate killings – is far more targeted than in Asia.

Hong Kong is a tolerant city. For Chinese people struggling with the reality of sexual orientation, the fallout from family and friends is in reality no different from anywhere else and in some cases, given the strength of family ties, can often be better. The community itself has in recent years come a long way in providing a network of advice and counselling. Groups such as Queer Straight Alliance and Community Business should be commended for this. Sexual orientation in the workplace is an issue that has come to prominence with the creation of diversity groups within multinational organisations which endeavour to cater for the needs of their complete workforce, and of course to stave off future litigation from a disgruntled employee. All these efforts have created a framework that allows LGBT people a place to seek guidance, friendship and companionship.

The government must of course increase its policies to include broadmindedness, acceptance and recognition for all its citizens, and LGBT is but a part of that. The city is a welcoming place to live and prosper. As a member of the LGBT community, I have found respect at many levels of society and believe Hong Kong to be a world-class city where diversity is accepted.

Mark Peaker, The Peak

11/06/2012

Why no official note for queen?

Could Hong Kong's government not have offered, on behalf of the people of Hong Kong, an official note of congratulations to celebrate the diamond jubilee of Queen Elizabeth?

The history of Hong Kong is entwined with the reign of this monarch, and even after 1997, the links between Hong Kong and England remain.

Mark Peaker, The Peak

Manipulation by Barclays defies belief

The manipulation of the London Interbank Offered Rate (Libor) by Barclays brings disrepute to the core of the British financial community.

It beggars belief that Bob Diamond, the bank's former chief executive who bestrode the financial crisis citing his bank's ability to navigate the tempest, knew nothing of his senior staff allowing practices of corruption to exist. His comment that traders' actions were "purely for their own benefit" is floored by the reality that his staff enacted illegal operations to boost their own profits as they sought to increase their own bonuses – which were ultimately agreed to by Mr Diamond.

These were not one-off trades by a rogue trader. Libor rates are calculated daily and published daily at 11am by the British Bankers' Association. It is the benchmark for setting interest rates. Barclays, as a high street lender, is a core component in the setting of Libor, and staff making up the contributing panel would have been aware of the actions of the dealing floor. Recorded phone conversations have revealed the complicity between traders and back-office staff.

The reliability of Libor is sacrosanct. It should have been calculated on the honest integrity of contributing banks from which loans were made to honest hard-working companies battling in the face of fiscal hardship.

As these small firms failed, Mr Diamond's staff were posting record profits. It is a moot point that Mr Diamond seems to be trying to state that their traders only manipulated the rate of Libor down or that "interventions in question were typically on the short term one and three-month Libor rates" which are generally only used by the wholesale market. It is moot because we don't know how far the manipulation of Libor has gone. It is moot because Libor should simply not have been manipulated.

It is deplorable for Mr Diamond to try to lay the blame on ministers or the Bank of England when he knew fully the consequences of making false Libor rates. Where was his integrity? The financial community used to be defined by the motto "dictum meum pactum", or "My word is my bond". It is time to redefine banking as a service industry that is there at the behest of the community to serve the needs of the community.

Mark Peaker, The Peak

02/08/2012

Stop excuses and get on with arts hub

Michael Lynch, CEO of the West Kowloon Cultural District Authority, informs us that the "basement is a complicated issue. It goes all under the site" ("Arts hub seeks more cash for basement", July 26).

Apparently, digging a hole in the ground now requires billions more in financing. I am perplexed, as I thought digging holes and making them into foundation areas normally incorporated creating basements. Was this overlooked in the Norman Foster plan? Was a basement an optional extra?

As the dilly-dallying continues, perhaps the authority needs reminding that the entire Marina Bay development in

Singapore and Guggenheim Museum, in Bilbao, Spain, were built in a fraction of the time it is taking to construct the arts hub. Both now are established art and cultural destinations.

All Hong Kong has is a fenced-off piece of reclaimed land. More than HK$21 billion has already been allocated to the project and to date nothing has been achieved other than the art of building bureaucracy.

Now we are told they need billions more to build a basement. It is outrageous and it is time to stop pussyfooting around and do what Hong Kong was once good at – building things.

Mark Peaker, The Peak

05/09/2012

Make sure idling engine ban obeyed

The government's ban on idling engines is effective only if Hong Kong drivers adhere to the law.

This will occur only when our police commence enforcing the law.

The ridiculous "three minutes per hour" wording in the December 2011 ordinance must be removed and no leeway should be allowed to drivers who do nothing but add to Hong Kong's air pollution.

Fines should be imposed on the spot and should be far in excess of the present HK$320. A more aggressive policing policy must be implemented. If Chief Executive Leung Chun-ying is true in his desire to clean Hong Kong's air, then he needs to do more than sit idly by.

Mark Peaker, The Peak

19/09/2012

Idling engine law proving ineffective

Hong Kong's idling engine legislation is perplexing as it is copied (according to an Environmental Protection Department official I spoke to) from the traffic and boat idling ordinance of Toronto, Canada.

It is bewildering because, in 2011, Toronto was officially ranked No. 1 city in the world in quality of living and clean air, and Hong Kong was voted one of the most polluted.

It is inexplicable that Hong Kong copies an environmental programme from a city that bears no resemblance to the problems the SAR [Special Administrative Region] suffers from.

Interestingly, the three minutes of permitted idling per 60 minutes was reduced in Toronto to just one minute and enforced regardless of the weather.

Hong Kong continues with its three minutes per hour, and should the hot weather signal be in effect, then idling for as long as you like is perfectly legal.

So, on days when pollutants should be reduced, our Environmental Protection Department allows empty coaches to idle and trucks to bellow noxious fumes into the air so a driver can sleep in his air-conditioned cabin.

It is a travesty of a law designed to appease the very people guilty of polluting our air; our government continues to treat the health of Hong Kong citizens as unimportant and this is simply not good enough.

Mark Peaker, The Peak

Look past Chao story for real gay issues

The hysterical offer by property tycoon Cecil Chao Sze-tsung to pay HK$500million for someone to marry his lesbian daughter should be taken with a pinch of salt. The response of gay rights activists to call upon the Equal Opportunities Commission to repair damage to Hong Kong's image is a drastic overreaction to an event that has far more to do with ostentatious wealth and vanity than the reality of being gay in Hong Kong.

As a gay businessman who speaks out publicly on lesbian, gay, bisexual and transgender (LGBT) issues, I am more concerned that an apparent "cornerstone of the Pink Season is the Mr Gay Hong Kong pageant" ("Chao's husband bounty 'blow to HK image'", September 30). This is also an event that should be taken with a pinch of salt; it tells the mainstream community that the gay community is frivolous and obsessed with image over substance when the community has worked tirelessly with corporations to ensure acceptance at all levels of society.

The recent surge in corporate acceptance of sexual diversity has allowed younger members of the LGBT community to work without persecution. There remains an immense amount of work to be done, especially for LGBT members who are not part of graduate trainee programmes but work in everyday jobs where such support does not exist.

Being gay is not a middle-class privilege, and the continued work for LGBT support networks must be to ensure that all persons, regardless of education and fiscal position, are allowed to develop their full potential free from fear and with a social support network to assist, train and educate all members of our society.

Mark Peaker, The Peak

Electrifying vision for city of the future

Environment secretary Wong Kam-sing's proposal to not renew the licences of diesel trucks more than 15 years of age is welcome, but why stop at one class of vehicle?

If boldness is what this new administration is about, then why not boldly go where no city has gone before and give Hong Kong 15 years to remove all combustion-engine vehicles from our roads? The rapid advancement of electric vehicles will easily accommodate the requirements of all traffic users.

Then Hong Kong can truly call itself a world-class city – the world's first all-electric metropolis, a city of the future.

Mark Peaker, The Peak

Threat of losing village unacceptable

The words of Cat Stevens' 1970 song "Where Do the Children Play?" could perhaps be adopted as the anthem for saving what is left of Hong Kong's natural beauty.

Hong Kong has indeed come a long way, we are changing day to day, but tell us, Chief Executive Leung Chun-ying, where do the children play?

The threat of losing Pak Sha O, home to 75 species of butterflies as well as numerous other animals, including rare and endangered species such as the Chinese softshell turtle and the hauntingly beautiful eagle owl, is simply unacceptable.

Built by the Hakka, Hong Kong's indigenous villagers, Pak Sha O represents our unique history. Allowing it to fall victim to development reflects an administration more in tune with corporate profit than community improvement.

Pak Sha O must be saved; it is Hong Kong's memory.

Mark Peaker, The Peak

Bright picture for flourishing arts scene

I refer to Roy Cuthbert's letter ("Artists need more space to exhibit", November 6). In the past two years there has been a significant increase in gallery space, especially around Wong Chuk Hang; 3812 Contemporary Art Projects has the island's largest space, with more than 7,000 square feet dedicated to Asian contemporary artists.

Also, Fine Art Asia, a Hong Kong-owned and -developed art fair, drew record international crowds last October for its annual fine art and antiques fair. Fine Art Asia also sponsors a hotel lobby exhibition twice a year where artists' works are displayed for the public to see.

K11 continues its excellent support and development of art and artists under the guidance of Adrian Cheng. The vibrancy of Hong Kong's art scene is developing, and this in turn is supporting local artists.

Para/Site continues its excellent work, and the recent addition of the Hong Kong Commercial Art Galleries Association brings a new level of distinction to Hong Kong's role as an international art hub.

Mark Peaker, co-founder and CEO, 3812 Contemporary Art Projects

02/12/2012

Synod's "no" vote a victory for bigotry

The recent vote by the General Synod to reject a 12-year campaign to allow women to be elevated to bishops has dealt a divisive blow to the heart of the Church of England.

Perhaps these bigoted bishops may now like to telephone Queen Elizabeth, head of the Church of England, and inform her that she is surplus to requirements.

Mark Peaker, The Peak

20/12/2012

Illegal parking law must be given teeth

The comment by Central and Western District councillor Cheng Lai-king that for wealthy people in Hong Kong, paying a parking "fine is just like paying a car-park fee" ("Chauffeurs more afraid of boss than parking fine", December 17) beggars belief.

He is effectively endorsing the right of tycoons to park wherever they like and merely pay a fine that matters little to them.

That the police are seen as secondary to bosses reflects the image of the police force that is mocked by drivers refusing to move because "my boss will yell at me".

Enforcement of illegal parking and idling in Hong Kong is laughable; the law needs to have teeth.

If drivers refuse to move, immediately arrest the driver and impound the car.

Perhaps then the owners may realise that the law comes first and the vanity of tycoons second.

Mark Peaker, The Peak

2013

Allow chief executive to get on with job

Hong Kong is a serious city with serious problems. It is time to cease this schoolyard bullying and focus on the issues that affect the daily lives of people who do not own numerous homes on The Peak or Kowloon Tong, but reside in subsidised housing that is smaller than the illegal structures in question.

Yes, Leung Chun-ying has gravely erred in his management of this but he was elected to do a job; let's allow him to continue with the good deeds he has achieved thus far.

His illegal structures are not acceptable, but neither is Henry Tang ying-yen now adding fuel to the fire as he sows the seeds for his eventual re-run for the chief executive position in 2017.

Hong Kong's leaders are the victims of their own vanity. It is time for the bickering to stop, and to get on with the serious business of making Hong Kong the city it should be and not the city we presently have.

Mark Peaker, The Peak

Government records must be in archive

It is heartening to read that the Ombudsman has finally yielded to pressure from Simon Chu Fook-keung, the former director of the Government Records Service (GRS) and others ("Call for archive law to protect valuable government data from loss", January 5).

Perhaps he realises that Hong Kong's lack of official archiving deprives our city of an essential legacy.

The fact that no official documents from the offices of the chief executive or the financial secretary have been transferred to the GRS ("since 1997") is not acceptable.

Correspondence from these offices is the intellectual property of Hong Kong. It is not for office holders to choose not to reveal records. Their thoughts and actions belong to the people.

If it was acceptable in 1084 for the Zizhi Tongjian to record a "Comprehensive Mirror to Aid in Government", then the writings of our leaders should mirror the running of a modern Hong Kong.

Mark Peaker, The Peak

Tang should give auction cash to charity

Henry Tang Ying-yen is auctioning off some of his collection of Burgundy ("Tang to part with fraction of wine collection", February 6).

He says that "after all, the best wines are shared".

One hopes, then, that the profit realised on his estimated HK$29 million windfall will be donated to charities as our former finance secretary shares his wealth with the poorer citizens of a city he tells us he cares about so deeply.

I think we can all toast to that.

Mark Peaker, The Peak

Culture hub poverty claims are an insult

Once again, Michael Lynch, the CEO of the West Kowloon Cultural District Authority, has failed to give accurate projections for the cost of building the first stage of the much anticipated and now largely ridiculed West Kowloon cultural hub ("Arts hub chief faces music over cost blowout", February 26).

Having made the contemptuous comment [in July of last year] that "the basement is a complicated thing; it goes all under the site ... It is complicated in financing", we are now informed of a massive miscalculation resulting in a HK$1.4 billion shortfall in the proposed building of the project's Xiqu Centre.

West Kowloon Cultural District was given an immensely generous endowment of HK$21.6 billion in 2008.
To put this into context, the Guggenheim Museum

Bilbao cost less than 10 per cent of this sum to build and was completed in a time frame of less than four years. The result is perhaps the world's most iconic art and cultural destination that has raised more than €500 million (HK$5 billion) for the city of Bilbao.

Frank Gehry's design forges a rare chemistry between design and the public. All this was achieved without massive cost overruns and in a timeline that delivered to the people what they wanted.

To date, West Kowloon Cultural District has delivered nothing other than bureaucracy and a proven inability to get the job done. Constantly complaining that almost US$2.8 billion is not enough money to build a cultural district is an affront to the people of Hong Kong.

It is time for Michael Lynch to stop begging and start building; the people of Hong Kong have simply had enough.

Mark Peaker, The Peak

Thatcher not only changed UK, but world

The death of Baroness Thatcher of Kesteven marks closure for a woman who galvanised not only her own generation, but those to come.

Loathed and loved with equal passion, Thatcher herself prized one thing more than any other – the success of Britain for all its citizens.

She never forgot her humble origins, nor the stern lessons of her father on the value of prudence – to balance the books and live within your means were the benchmarks of her life.

Thatcher was more a classical liberal than the Tory she will be remembered for. Indeed, Thatcher herself commented in 1983 that "I would not mind betting that if [former prime minister William] Gladstone were alive today he would apply to join the Conservative Party".

A conviction politician who was "not for turning", she led the United Kingdom through a period of economic turmoil and trade union warfare. She was a unique yet divisive person who changed not only Britain, but the world. She will be remembered with passion, and history shall judge her as one of our greatest leaders.

May she rest in peace with her beloved Denis, and may we be grateful for the freedoms her foresight allowed us to enjoy.

Mark Peaker, The Peak

Denunciation of Thatcher ignores facts

I refer to Michael Waugh's letter ("Good riddance to architect of greed cult", April 12) in reply to me ("Thatcher not only changed UK, but world", April 10). I am thankful to him for his damnation of me along with Margaret Thatcher – to be compared to her is glorious.

To correct his rather naive view that Thatcher "caused the demise of British manufacturing", let us look at the facts. It is hard to exaggerate the pitiful state of Britain in the 1970s. Edward Heath's reckless economic policy left a legacy of high inflation.

The Labour administrations of Harold Wilson and James Callaghan made things worse. A refusal to accept that Britain could not spend its way out of trouble led to the International Monetary Fund having to rescue the country from bankruptcy in 1976.

The private sector was held hostage by the unions.

The country was paralysed by a rail strike, National Health Service employees worked to rule and ambulance drivers went on strike. Rubbish went uncollected and most infamous of all was the strike of gravediggers in Liverpool, which led to the dead going unburied and coffins piling up.

When Thatcher won office, she delivered on her promises. Having emasculated the unions by bringing them within the law, she was able to proceed with the strategy of restructuring the economy and dragging Britain into the 20th century.

As a result, not only was the country transformed, but so was our standing in the world and our ability to believe in ourselves and to compete.

Mark Peaker, The Peak

Pumping up culture hub a big let-down

I refer to the piece in Lai See ("New cultural district to inflate interest with bouncy Stonehenge", April 24).

How deflated must West Kowloon Cultural District be as some of their bouncy castles have been punctured. It would appear M+ curator Lars Nittve's grandiose description, "monumentality, temporariness and permanence, as well as beauty and the grotesque" has indeed been achieved.

I wonder if pumps and a bicycle repair kit were included.

Mark Peaker, The Peak

Snowden saga reveals true human nature

Edward Snowden has revealed what we all know – that governments spy.

Whilst we all happily watch 007 and Jason Bourne and marvel at their antics, we take affront when the faceless reach of any government invades our own privacy.

Of course, this is nothing new. The desire to know what someone else is thinking has always existed; a family member's diary or a partner's WhatsApp account may often reveal secrets; of course, this is petty when compared to the international hacking of agencies from foreign governments reading a citizen's private communication, but the desire is the same.

Mr Snowden has revealed a human weakness that, in an age of a billion messages an hour, is too tempting to ignore. Morally and legally wrong? Yes; but human nature nonetheless.

Mark Peaker, The Peak

16/07/2013

Club linked with Hong Kong's growth

As the storm clouds gather over the hallowed fairways of Fanling, one can but ponder the thoughts of members facing the closure of their beloved club.

It is easy to mock the Hong Kong Golf Club as a privileged bastion available only to the few, but the club is more than this; with a history entwined with the growth of Hong Kong, the club and its elder members represent a part of our heritage and cannot be so easily set asunder.

Hong Kong Golf Club can be part of a new generation of golfers who aspire to the best, and the club's outreach programmes aim to achieve this; if we reclaim all our land for development, tell me, where do our children play?

Mark Peaker, The Peak

Stadium pitch fix shouldn't be outsourced

I refer to the recent round of mud-slinging as a result of the less-than-perfect pitch at Hong Kong Stadium.

Why does it take an overseas consultant, ironically from New Zealand, a country more famed for land erosion as a result of massive deforestation, to tell our hapless Leisure and Cultural Services Department that the pitch needs improved aeration and drainage? How revealing.

Chief Secretary Carrie Lam Cheng Yuet-ngor visited Singapore to see how our once lesser competitor has for 10 years run rings around Hong Kong in terms of cultural and sport development. She may have found that Singapore trains local people who are talented, and who are connected to and have a passion for their city.

Surely given the millions who live in Hong Kong we can find the same talent and stop outsourcing at vast expense the jobs that Hong Kong people should be able to do, and do with pride.

Mark Peaker, The Peak

Idling engine ban law is ineffective

The Hong Kong government could not care less about the quality of Hong Kong's air.

This is evident in the laughable enforcement of illegally parked cars which spend their entire days idling, free of fear of prosecution.

On days when the very hot weather signal is in effect, these drivers can legally sit for hours on end idling away in air-conditioned comfort, adding to the city's air pollution totally secure in the knowledge the law is on their side. How can this be the policy of a government concerned with the air we all have to breathe?

That the Environmental Protection Department and police enforcement of illegal parking and illegal idling is incompetently pursued is no longer news. That the government of Leung Chun-ying continues to look the other way and allow this illegal activity to continue unabated reflects his own nefarious neglect of Hong Kong people's right to clean air.

Mark Peaker, The Peak

01/09/2013

Criticism of golf club is out of bounds

Tommy F. K. Hui's letter regarding the Hong Kong Golf Club is wholly unfair ("Hong Kong Golf Club has done little to help budding talents", August 25).

While the club may need to improve its outreach to the broader community (I stress I am not a member), Mr Hui's accusations that club members look on "with disapproving eyes" and day guests are restricted from going "here there and everywhere" is incorrect.

I have played at the club, either as a member's guest or with other non-member friends, numerous times over the past decade. I can attest that the welcome from other members and from the club's staff is nothing less than courteous.

Clearly Mr Hui feels the need to be treated as a VIP. Perhaps, then, it is his attitude and not the club's that needs addressing.

Mark Peaker, The Peak

Better care for elderly left to exist in misery

"Age shall not weary them nor the years condemn" is an affectionate remembrance for those taken in youth; for the rest, age does weary and the years do condemn; it is a path that awaits us all.

As Hong Kong's rapidly ageing population grows, so do the pressures upon families who must care for elderly relatives while balancing the emotional and fiscal burden of their own lives.

As living spaces in Hong Kong become smaller, and as wives, often the surrogate nurse, need to work and care for children, the pressure on the elderly increases. Hong Kong's insufficient old age homes provide merely for existence and not for the remaining life the elderly have a right to enjoy.

Having taken the journey of my mother's own stroke and rehabilitation over the past few years, I have seen the lack of provision for the elderly in Hong Kong. Dementia is a topic which has recently been highlighted by the case of Alzheimer's sufferer Professor Charles Kao, winner of the Nobel Prize for physics and the father of fibre optics. It is a problem facing many Hong Kong families today.

While old age does not necessarily lead to dementia, our elderly is at greater risk of getting this disorder, which undermines the very being of that person, robbing them of their character and their independence. This often results in family decay and financial devastation.

The linkage between dementia and old age poverty must not be overlooked. The outreach to the elderly community by the government must be improved. The elderly has a right to quality care, and families need to know that financial, medical and social support exists.

Mark Peaker, The Peak

Shanghai trade zone sends a wake-up call

Chief Executive Leung Chun-ying is correct that the new free-trade zone in Shanghai will not "threaten" Hong Kong, but it most certainly will challenge it.

Li Ka-shing's more prudent observation that the zone "will have a big impact on Hong Kong" reflects that the city needs to stop feeling sorry for itself and start focusing on the real handover in 2047 when the SAR [Special Administrative Region] ceases to be and Hong Kong likely becomes fully integrated with the mainland.

The central government has been meticulous in observing the terms of the Joint Declaration and allowed Hong Kong to go about its business.

Competition on a global scale defined this city, yet across the border in Shenzhen, 11 million people work; a bridge to Macau and Zhuhai will soon bring the other side of this pincer movement closer.

Megacities such as Chengdu, Tianjin, Ningbo, Wuhan and even Taipei will continue to compete against one another and against Hong Kong. With a population of less than 10 million, Hong Kong risks becoming no more than a suburb; it is not on track for 2047.

Neglecting to plan for a future deemed too far away to worry about may be Hong Kong's ultimate failing.

Hong Kong must define its own place, export its own excellence and prepare for a role in a vastly different future. The changes in Shanghai should be seen as the first warning shot across the bow that Hong Kong needs to find its long-term competitive advantage within the larger nation it is part of.

Mark Peaker, The Peak

Resurgent China has vibrant cities

Anson Chan Fang On-sang makes poignant comments about the future of Hong Kong, a city she and all of us call home ("HK must set role in developing the nation, says Chan", October 28).

However, her statement that "we don't want Hong Kong to turn into another Chinese city" is derogatory in that it makes the assumption that Chinese cities are inferior.

Is this true of cities such as Beijing, Shanghai, Ningbo, Chengdu and Tianjin?

All these cities are redefining themselves for the role they will play in the future of a resurgent China. Hong Kong, with its unique past, must learn to adapt to a future where its skills and expertise continue to make the city relevant for its future incorporation into the fabric of the motherland.

This requires more than a slogan that pretentiously claims us to be "Asia's world city".

Expectations raised and then not fulfilled lead to criticism every time and we are no different from other places.

Hong Kong requires corporate, social and political leaders, not procrastinators, to overcome the challenges we face and for our city to proudly take its place as "a city within China".

Mark Peaker, The Peak

Threat of sanctions must now be lifted

As the Philippines mourns the deaths of thousands of its citizens, perhaps it is time for Hong Kong to reach out and aid a country that serves this city daily. Sanctions must be forgotten and the arm of friendship extended.

It is time for humanity to heal the hurt that both peoples have suffered.

Mark Peaker, The Peak

KMB buses seem to come all at once

Perhaps KMB [Kowloon Motor Bus Co.] might like to explain why there are often two or three of their buses following one another on the same route, each one virtually empty.

Profitable bus firms, like any company, avoid duplication to reduce costs. Perhaps KMB might want to help themselves, the congestion they cause and the air they pollute, by paying more attention to operations and less to demands for more money for a fleet that is badly managed.

Mark Peaker, The Peak

2014

Use surplus to install smoke detectors

The fire in the 24-storey Continental Mansion, in North Point, on Sunday once again reflects the need for smoke detectors to be mandatory in all buildings in Hong Kong.

In a city where almost everyone lives in high-rise accommodation, it is only a matter of time before a towering inferno will claim lives that might otherwise have been saved.

Perhaps spending a fraction of the government's ridiculous surplus to prevent loss of life might be considered money well spent.

Mark Peaker, The Peak

Do more to protect us all from fire risk

I refer to the letter by Pang Chi-ming ("Some older buildings are beyond help", January 13) in reply to my letter ("Use surplus to install smoke detectors", January 1) on the installation of smoke detectors in all buildings.

He needs to know that modern smoke detectors are wireless, they are simply attached to a wall or ceiling and battery-operated.

Individual unit costs are not high, and for families on restricted incomes, the government should install and pay.

For all new developments, it should be mandatory for all new builds to be fitted with smoke detectors.

Our government should be doing far more to protect its citizens from fire. It requires nothing more than a cheap detector unit, but perhaps life is considered cheaper.

Mark Peaker, The Peak

Traffic police incapable of enforcing law

The use of hand-held mobile phones by taxi drivers is hardly news, accustomed as we are to dashboards resembling the bridge of the Starship Enterprise, with the driver deftly fielding calls as passengers sit mesmerised in the back.

I encountered this on Garden Road last year, where a driver had nine phones affixed to the dashboard. At one point, we were flanked by two Klingon battleships, otherwise known as Hong Kong traffic police, who could clearly see my "captain" illegally using hand-held devices. Their reaction was to activate their cloaking devices and disappear.

While I make light of this, dangerous driving in Hong Kong is on the rise. The comment by the police that they "collect information on this" reflects their overall lethargic attitude to motoring offences and their inability to enforce the law.

Mark Peaker, The Peak

Angered by top official's arrogance

The condescending letter from Christine Loh Kung-wai, undersecretary for the environment ("Green group wrong about bad air days", March 3), shows her disdain for anyone who questions her; that she ends the letter "air science is complicated" reflects her attitude.

The only complication in Hong Kong's filthy air is the ineptitude of her department and its failure to curb roadside, shipping and other pollutants that require nothing more than enforcement. But why risk losing your job by being effective when, after all, playing politics "is complicated"?

Mark Peaker,
The Peak

Stop ranting about electoral process

I refer to the letter by David Hall ("Urging public nomination a distraction", March 12).

Mr Hall highlights a core reality in the puerile demands of those seeking election of our chief executive via universal suffrage.

It should be remembered that British Prime Minister David Cameron garnered only 36.1 per cent of the popular vote in 2010 and rules now only by an alliance with a party that came last in the polls [of the three main parties].

As Mr Hall correctly states, it is "a fallacy that universal suffrage is synonymous with public nomination of candidates". Hong Kong faces a vastly different future, one ruled ultimately by the capital city of the country that Hong Kong is a part of, China.

Broader representation from the community to ensure key issues are heard is important, and one hopes that future chief executives will be elected from a wider nominating committee. But regardless of the size of the committee, the fact remains that any chief executive will oversee Hong Kong as a city within China.

Rather than rant and rave about the fallacy of the process, we need to focus on the issues facing Hong Kong and our city's role within a resurgent China; let us remember that 2047 is not very far away at all.

Mark Peaker, The Peak

Why keeping records is important

The report by Howard Winn in Lai See regarding this administration's ineptness in ensuring Hong Kong's archives are actually archived reflects accurately the dismal state of our civil service ("Yet another damning report on government archives", March 21).

That our government bureaus are staffed by a motley collection of lethargic salary people who have neither the gumption nor inclination and certainly little passion for their jobs is reflected in the dire state of a civil service that finds itself the farcical image of *Yes Minister*.

The Government Records Service seems to have failed to grasp that archiving is vital to the foundation of any civilised society. These documents are the tangible memory of Hong

Kong, they belong to future generations, which will want to know just how Hong Kong was managed.

Perhaps therein lies the rub. Are we so ashamed of our inability to run this city that it is better to discard the documents?

Mark Peaker, The Peak

22/04/2014

Students' threat of action is immature

I refer to the report ("Ignore us and we'll occupy: students", April 16).

The puerile demands of the student-led activist group Scholarism and the Federation of Students' warning, as they tabled a joint reform proposal for the 2017 election, reflects more the mentality of the pram than the logic of intellectuals – don't give us what we want and we will sulk and occupy.

In their own words, "If the government rejects such a proposal, which could be endorsed by 100,000 residents, that would be [tantamount] to trampling on public opinion and insulting the public."

In a city of seven million, when did 100,000 become the majority? These young people can be admired for their courage to voice an opinion; however, their demands are flawed and immature.

Hong Kong is simply another city within China.

Armed with the benefit of an education, these students should be embracing the opportunities presented to them by a resurgent China. To imagine that our colonial past gives us a right to special treatment is folly.

Rather than waste energy on futile debate about a chief executive and 2017, the argument should be where Hong

Kong will be in 2047 when the real challenge to our city's ability to be relevant within China will matter.

Mark Peaker, The Peak

Traffic wardens failing to act

I refer to the letter by Ken McGowan ("Zigzag lines help protect pedestrians", May 5).

He is absolutely correct that frequent parking on what is supposed to be a restricted zone will result, eventually, in loss of life.

He refers to enforcement of the law [on pedestrian crossings] in Britain. In London, there exists an army of traffic enforcement officers who do exactly what their job description entails.

In Hong Kong, we have the laziest traffic enforcement force.

It is probably easier to observe an enforcement officer zigzag his way to avoid doing his job than see an offending motorist actually fined for illegal parking.

Mark Peaker, The Peak

Impressive philanthropic track record

I refer to the letter from William Stevenson Spencer ("Hong Kong does not need Li Ka-shing", May 14).

Mr Spencer's accusations are unfounded. It makes no sense to cite the daily changing prices of goods on the supermarket shelf as a core reason to denigrate a man who has donated billions to Hong Kong and mainland universities as well as to health care development.

Li Ka-shing is not obsessed with lining his own pockets, his investments in companies such as Facebook could have poured billions back into his private accounts; rather, the money flows purely to the Li Ka Shing Foundation and the numerous worthy causes it supports.

Should Li Ka-shing decide to leave Hong Kong, the city will survive, as it will should Mr Spencer decide to leave. The difference is that Li Ka-shing will leave a legacy of philanthropy that has benefited the people.

Mark Peaker, The Peak

Cathay's idea of bidding for upgrade great

The scheme Cathay Pacific is considering to allow passengers to bid for vacant seats in premium economy and business class is an excellent idea ("Cathay considers seat upgrade auction", May 30).

It gives any person the opportunity to purchase a premium seat at a competitive price and allows the airline to fly without empty seats. It reflects Cathay's competence in revenue generation and reminds those who see upgrades as a right that it is in fact a privilege.

If passengers cannot abide being behind the curtain, now there is a way to sit in front – pay for it.

Mark Peaker, The Peak

20/06/2014

Help for the elderly there on request

In reply to L. C. Wong's letter ("Cathay Pacific baggage policy hard to bear", June 18), Cathay Pacific will always, upon request, ensure any elderly passenger is well looked after.

A ground staff member will meet an elderly passenger, especially if he or she is travelling with a medical condition, and ensure baggage is collected from the carousel and loaded on to a trolley, and will escort the passenger to the point of immigration – all this has been provided for my elderly mother free of charge.

Cathay Pacific does not seek to profit from the elderly. Had the passenger's condition been clearly explained, L. C. Wong's father would have been treated in the same manner and he would never have had to lift a 23kg bag himself.

Mark Peaker, The Peak

17/07/2014

Revealing Patten's true loyalties

Brian Stuckey states in his letter his endearing support for our former governor Lord Patten ("Britain turns blind eye to white paper", July 11).

How misguided his view is evidenced by his belief that while Patten was governor, he served the needs of Hong Kong people over and above the aspirations of Westminster. Patten does of course share a common thread with Beijing; he was never elected by the people of Hong Kong and ruled over the fading vestiges of colonial power in the territory. He was given the post to make up for his humiliating election defeat in his constituency in Britain.

Beijing is Hong Kong's ruler, as London once was; cities are subservient to the countries that rule them. Patten has spent his career being loyal and should remember this before he needlessly seeks to stir sentiment.

Mark Peaker, The Peak

28/07/2014

MTR Corp is clearly on the right track

As the continued debate about 2017 rages and Scholarism threatens to occupy Central, damaging our city's international reputation, it was heartening to see that the recently maligned MTR Corporation had secured a significant contract in the UK ("MTR wins £1.4b contract to run London Crossrail", July 19).

Awarding this contract to a Hong Kong company reflects the true spirit and capability of this city and perhaps reminds all of us what we should be focusing on – the ability to run world-class, locally grown businesses that compete on a global playing field.

Hong Kong is a city filled with talent and an entrepreneurial spirit.

It can compete with any city within China and the rest of the world, and it is here that our focus should be.

Clearly the MTR Corp is on the right track.

Mark Peaker, The Peak

Many failing to treat domestic helpers fairly

That some maids from Bangladesh and Myanmar are returning home only months after arriving, aggravating a shortage of domestic helpers, reflects also the appalling expectations placed upon them, and on the much larger Philippine foreign domestic helper community.

It is easy for those of us who employ foreign domestic helpers to criticise their job ability, but spend little time looking at how we, as supposedly responsible employers, treat them. It is time for the government to look at the requirements of those who seek to employ domestic help.

If an apartment is below a certain size, for example, 1,000 square foot, or if any sized apartment cannot offer separate living quarters for a domestic helper, then that person cannot be permitted to employ a helper.

I am disheartened to hear of helpers being forced to sleep inside cupboards, or on towels on kitchen floors. In one case I heard of, the maid was forced to clean and shower at the local community centre because her employers' 450 square foot apartment had only one bathroom and they would not let her use it.

New controls implemented by the government are required. A person cannot justify the employment of a maid simply because they don't like cleaning their own toilet. All domestic helpers are human and many are proud wage earners for their families. They deserve respect and it is time to stop the basic slavery many Hong Kong families make them endure.

Mark Peaker, The Peak

Enforcement of the law laughable

David Akers-Jones' comment regarding "professors giving advice to our schoolchildren about how they can boycott classes" accurately portrays part of a larger problem in Hong Kong, that of enforcement of the law.

Chief Secretary Carrie Lam Cheng Yuet-ngor has tried, wisely, to tell students not to risk their futures by getting criminal convictions.

Yet students are confident about engaging in civil disobedience and breaking the law because they believe they shall get away with it. Enforcement of the law in Hong Kong has become laughable, from the plethora of illegally parked cars to the rioting of students who threaten the very future of our city.

Hong Kong is a peaceful city that enjoys all of the freedoms guaranteed under the Sino-British Joint Declaration that set out the terms of Hong Kong's return to Chinese sovereignty.

We need stronger enforcement of the laws that have kept this city non-violent and prosperous or we risk losing everything because an anti-establishment group of vocal protesters, who still have their underwear washed and ironed by their mothers, feel they are invincible.

Mark Peaker, The Peak

Protest has now become intimidation

The siege of vital arteries of our city continues to cause great discomfort and stress to the majority of Hong Kong citizens who have a right to go about their lives unimpeded.

London, New York, Tokyo or Berlin, all capitals of great democracies, would never allow their cities to be blockaded for over a week; this is no longer a protest, it is intimidation.

It is time for Hong Kong to stop being held hostage to these unreasonable students who do not represent any majority whatsoever.

Mark Peaker, The Peak

30/10/2014

Loudspeaker needed round the clock at site

Images of protesters emerging from their tents after a sound night's sleep, as citizens continue to be inconvenienced, convey the smug attitude of those who continue to hold our city hostage.

Surely it is time for a low-flying police helicopter and some 24-hour loudspeaker announcements, all of course to assist the safety of these children, for surely, we would not wish to inconvenience them and rouse them too early from their slumber.

Mark Peaker,
The Peak

Protesters are ignoring majority view

I refer to the letter by Anthony Wong Yiu-ming ("Police must work to restore public trust after tear gas attack", November 7).

To claim the police used tear gas against students without provocation reflects his own biased and ignorant view of the facts of that moment.

Police reacted to violent physical and verbal threats against them. Perhaps he would like to stand still while a ranting mob thrust umbrella points into his face.

If he so abhors violence, perhaps he can explain why the main barricade in Connaught Road is reinforced with sharpened bamboo poles that would mutilate anyone who fell into it. Is this the action of a non-violent protest group?

As with the rest of his motley assortment of protesters, he demands this and demands that with scant respect for the law or the facts and total disregard of the view of the majority of Hong Kong people.

Mark Peaker, The Peak

Cathay takes good care of travelling pets

Seth Rogen's ferocious attack on Cathay Pacific reflects a typical arrogance one expects from an overindulged actor accustomed to getting his own way.

As he provided no details as to why Cathay refused to allow his dog to be carried, we can assume it was owing to him not completing the required documents or the animal not being correctly vaccinated.

Having travelled from Hong Kong to Vancouver several times with dogs carried, I can attest to the outstanding service Cathay provides, the animals arriving in excellent condition.

International airlines have strict guidelines to stop the spread of dangerous diseases should the animal not be properly vaccinated; regardless of who the owner is, everyone must comply with this.

Clearly Rogen feels himself above the rest of us and I am grateful that his intimidation of Cathay staff was not sufficient to sway an airline dedicated to service and safety, for humans and for canines!

Mark Peaker, The Peak

2015

Local talent can do the job, Mr Leung

Our chief executive's decision, in the policy address, that Hong Kong needs to hire more overseas talent baffles many.

In a city of seven million people, perhaps he and his government should do more to bolster the opportunities for the abundance of talent that exists within Hong Kong. This is talent that, unlike the imported foreigner, is trilingual and a part of the fabric of our society. And these are people who are not likely to amass a small fortune from inflated bonuses and rent-free accommodation and then depart.

As an employer, I grow tired of receiving curricula vitae from want-to-be expatriates who claim they can deliver so much "international experience" but cannot speak a word of the local language and have a dearth of knowledge about Hong Kong or China.

Senior CEOs hired for government-led infrastructure projects in Hong Kong in recent years exemplify this. Members of the community who are meant to be the beneficiaries of these projects would not even know the names of these foreigners, who, in return, know nothing of the sentiment of the city because they are so shielded from it.

Perhaps our government should look at importing foreign civil service talent.

It could hire someone from a traffic department who understands that illegally parked cars are a problem, or from a fire department who would be puzzled as to why Hong Kong developers are not obliged to fit smoke detectors in all apartments. Or perhaps we could get a mayor who understands that to serve the people, you must first listen to them.

Mark Peaker, The Peak

31/01/2015

A crime unpunished is one too many

I refer to the letter from Steve Hui Chun-tak, chief superintendent of the police public relations branch, in which he defends the actions of his police force in combating drug crime in Lan Kwai Fong ("Committed to curbing drug dealers", January 27).

It is of note that Hong Kong police are very quick to release numbers of what they have accomplished in terms of drug raids, parking tickets, illegal idling and parking enforcement, but never accept criticism that more needs to be done. One suspects that an illegally parked car around Lan Kwai Fong, its engine idling as its driver waits for his drug-dealing passenger, is unlikely to get booked, unless, of course, the dealer jaywalks. Boasting about success is not correct when illegal activity continues to be, for the greater part, ignored by Hong Kong police, who seemingly turn a blind eye to numerous breaches of the law that impact the daily lives of Hong Kong citizens.

Mark Peaker, The Peak

Baffling move to chop more heritage

Yet again our hapless civil servants, in this case the Secretary for Development, Chan Mo-po, and the Director of Water Supplies, Lam Tin-sing, demonstrate a complete lack of comprehension for the quality of air in Hong Kong and a blatant disregard for our city's heritage.

Perhaps they would like to explain how the felling of 118 trees in Hong Kong Park's wooded slope and the destruction of a major section of the 150-year-old squared rubble defensive wall of Flagstaff House reflects the government's so-called campaign to allow Hong Kong to breathe and to preserve what little architectural heritage we have left ("Pumped up over heritage", February 4)?

The loss of the trees would impact the function of Hong Kong Park as our city's "lungs", easing air pollution and providing a well-ventilated place where citizens can relax. Flagstaff House and its grounds, including the old stone wall and classical balustrade, should be permanently conserved as a monument.

The need to spend HK$750 million of taxpayers' money for the relocation of the pumping station is folly, given the existing water pumping station is in good order and can be retained or reconfigured in situ to allow 21,000 square metres of commercial floor area to be built on top.

The relocation of the pumping station will impact 2,150 square metres of park space, effectively lost. This is not in the interest of Hong Kong citizens – it is purely for the benefit of civil servants to be seen to be doing something.

Mark Peaker, The Peak

Some helpers face cramped living space

The jailing of Law Wan-tung for abusing her domestic helper Erwiana Sulistyaningsih is a welcome result.

This case will call into question the law requiring domestic helpers to live with their employers. However, there is a larger issue that needs debating: this being whether Hong Kong needs this absurd reliance on domestic helpers to clean apartments when it fails to offer secure and private accommodation for them. It is inhumane for any employer to force a person to sleep on the floor, in a cupboard or in a child's room. It removes from the domestic helper their sense of dignity and independence.

It is a comprehensive failure on behalf of the government that no checks are maintained to ensure helpers have the actual accommodation specified on the application form; it is time for this to stop. Owners of apartments under a certain size and without dedicated accommodation for helpers should be barred from hiring domestic staff. Perhaps the time has come for Hong Kong people to start cleaning their own toilet.

Mark Peaker, The Peak

Lee's views on democracy profound

Lee Kuan Yew was the outstanding Asian statesman of his generation.

It is true that he imposed his austere, incorruptible and often dislikeable persona on Singapore life, yet stability and economic progress were, for him, unequivocally higher priorities than Western notions of freedom.

In a withering attack on Chris Patten, he derided the then newly arrived governor for his views on democratic reform.

He said: "I have never believed that democracy brings progress. I know it to have brought regression. I watch it year by year, and it need not have been thus."

Perhaps these are words we should continue to reflect upon in Hong Kong.

Mark Peaker, The Peak

Pan-dems should heed public interest

As the pan-democrats squirm and wiggle in their opposition to any electoral reform other than their own agenda ("Public support on 2017 'will not sway pan-dems'", April 24), perhaps they should glance at the abandonment of the Federation of Students and realise how quickly popular support can turn, as yet another university votes to withdraw ("Shaky times ahead as third pull-out hits Federation", April 24).

Unlike the pan-democrats, the Federation's mature new secretary general, Nathan Law Kwun-chung, seemingly understands that it may have to change.

He said: "We have to face the question: Is the Federation still representative? What does it stand for?"

This is a question the pan-democrats should be asking themselves as they risk Hong Kong's future stability based upon their own selfish interests. Rather than seek harmony and a way to move forward that will benefit everyone, all they offer is continued disruption, along with their resident mob superstar Joshua Wong Chi-fung, who said his group planned more protests.

Democracy works both ways and those who seek to exploit it for their own vanity are soon brought to heel.

Mark Peaker, The Peak

14/05/2015

Police lethargic about illegal parking

The news that the HK$320 fixed penalty for illegal parking could be raised for the first time in 21 years, possibly to HK$448, as part of measures authorities are considering to tackle road congestion, is laughable.

Our police and traffic wardens take a lethargic attitude when it comes to imposing existing laws that prohibit illegal parking.

This complete lack of enforcement makes a mockery of any revision to the actual cost of the infringement.

If the Transport and Housing Bureau really wishes to improve congestion on our roads, it needs to demand that our traffic laws are enforced, that police officers who meekly appear subservient to tycoon drivers don't simply wave the offending car on only for it to reappear once it has driven around the block.

Also, those drivers who reoffend should lose points from their licence.

Hong Kong deserves better than the car park it has become, and our citizens deserve the right to walk on pavements free of obstruction.

The cost of the fine is irrelevant; it is the lack of police enforcement that is the issue.

Mark Peaker, The Peak

Same-sex unions should be legal in HK

Ireland's resounding referendum to legalise gay marriage in the world's first national vote on the issue is remarkable for its enlightenment.

For this devoutly Catholic society to deliver to the world a result that recognises all its citizens, regardless of sexual orientation, with equality, reflects an affirmation of the views of young people who seek a future free from bigotry.

Hong Kong must now live up to its self-appointed mantle as "Asia's world city" and recognise same-sex unions.

Late last year, a survey by the Family School Sexual Orientation Discrimination Ordinance Concern Group found that around 70 per cent of Hongkongers believe it is okay for people to be anti-homosexual.

This jaundiced poll, that represented the views of a tiny group of 611 persons, was not reflective of the younger generation which wishes to see Hong Kong prosper as a city where any form of discrimination is not tolerated.

Those who argue that homosexuality is not part of the culture of the traditional Chinese family are wrong. The existence of homosexuality in China has been well documented since ancient times in both writing and art.

The people of Ireland have struck a massive blow against discrimination, and Oscar Wilde would be proud of his country today.

It is now time for Hong Kong to make us proud and recognise the contribution the lesbian, gay, bisexual, transgender community, free from judgement, can make to our city's future.

Mark Peaker, The Peak

25/06/2015

Appalled by lawmakers' ignorance

The sheer embarrassment of the fiasco that was the supposed historic vote for democracy in Hong Kong brings to light the utter incompetence of all Legco members, and they must take full responsibility for the humiliation they have brought.

The decision by 31 lawmakers to try and delay procedures to wait for Lau Wong-fat shows ignorance of the rules of the Legco chamber.

Lawmakers need to take a hard look at themselves and realise they are meant to be there for the betterment of Hong Kong and not for their own vanity.

The next step for democracy is for the people of Hong Kong to return to the chamber representatives who serve us.

Mark Peaker, The Peak

Long history of homosexuality in China

I refer to the letter by Peter Wei ("Same-sex marriage not right for HK", July 2).

He says, "according to tradition in China, a country with a long history, it would be against the yin/yang principle not to observe the 'one man, one woman' marriage system". This shows his ignorance of his own cultural history.

Chinese historical data provided by ancient records dealing with male homosexuality dates back to the Shang dynasty (second millennium BC), according to Professor Li Yinhe in her study of the history of Chinese homosexuality.

The term *luan feng* was used to describe homosexuality in the "Shang Dynasty Records", and there are historical records of male homosexuality persistently through the different dynasties, from ancient times to the present day.

When he cites religious beliefs that Christians believe homosexuals shall not enter heaven, he is expressing views that are no longer representative of the majority of people who have the maturity and wisdom to understand that inclusive love is far better than divisive beliefs. This is aptly recognised in Ireland, a predominantly Catholic society, and now in the United States.

Peter Wei concludes with "the harms caused by same-sex marriage are too many to enumerate".

Let me assure him that the benefits of an accepting society, united by its diversity, where love replaces discrimination and tolerance replaces intolerance, are indeed too many to enumerate.

Mark Peaker, The Peak

20/07/2015

Standing firm in defence of free society

David Webb is renowned for his fastidious attention to detail and his unabashed lack of humility in challenging points that many feel unnecessary.

Hearing him in full oratorical prowess is something to behold. His present battle with the Privacy Commissioner for Personal Data reflects his commitment to stand firm for what is right ("'Orwellian' risk of deleting names from website", July 14).

He is to be commended for not caving in to the pressures applied that seek to benefit the few at the expense of the many. A tangled web indeed but one that prevents the Orwellian abuse of Hong Kong's much-heralded free and open society.

Mark Peaker, The Peak

07/08/2015

Hong Kong definitely still has a heart

There has been much comment recently of how selfish Hong Kong people have become.

It is not an entirely false observation, especially among those who believe their view is the only view.

However, we can be assured that this selfishness exists within a minority and Hong Kong is a place where caring for others still exists.

This has recently been so warmly shown with the family of Cheng Chi-ming and his daughters' bravery in offering part of their livers to save their father in a world-first simultaneous liver operation. To paraphrase the recently departed Cilla Black, "Hong Kong has a heart."

Mark Peaker, The Peak

18/08/2015

Cabbies have themselves to blame

How amusing that the police reacted to the powerful taxi lobby with undercover police arresting several Uber drivers while raiding the company's office.

One wonders when the last undercover operation took place to arrest illegal behaviour of taxi drivers who use dangerously maintained vehicles with banks of phones attached to their dashboards, and who overcharge passengers and refuse to go to destinations they feel are not profitable enough.

The reason for the rise of Uber can be found with taxi drivers themselves; Hong Kong people are fed up with poor service offered by rude drivers in filthy cars who often drive with scant regard to safety.

Uber is a breath of fresh air in a market dominated by self-interest and competes by offering better service.

Mark Peaker, The Peak

Repression of gays hurts economies

I refer to the letter by Ndemio Stephane ("Gay rights simply not an issue in Kenya", August 17).

If gay rights are not an issue, what then of human rights? Is your correspondent who says that "people who cannot change their sexual preference, then they can go live where homosexuality is legal" an advocate of forcing people to deny who they are? Does he condone Kenya's new anti-homosexuality bill recently submitted by the Republican Party in the National Assembly that will allow [foreign] gay people in Kenya to be sentenced to death by stoning?

Ndemio Stephane is ignorant of the reality of the lives of countless numbers of Kenyans who are discriminated against, stigmatised and subjected to torture, often resulting in death, because of their sexual orientation.

They face arbitrary arrest and unnecessary harassment by the police who extort money from them, and they are only released after bribing their way out of custody.

Your reader's comment of asking if a country will advance economically if it embraces gay rights is easily answered: yes, it does.

A report released in November 2014 by the United States Agency for International Development and the Williams Institute at the University of California Los Angeles found that countries that treat lesbian, gay, bisexual, transgender [LGBT] people equally have better-performing economies.

A study of 39 countries compared a measure of rights granted by each nation related to homosexuality, decriminalisation, non-discrimination laws and family rights to gross domestic product [GDP] per capita and other measures of economic performance.

The positive link between rights and development was clear: countries that come closer to full equality for LGBT people have higher levels of GDP per capita.

Diversity is a part of humanity, and the views of this correspondent and the Kenyan government reflect their failure to be a part of it.

Mark Peaker, The Peak

Scout for local talent to run arts hub

The pending departure of Lars Nittve, executive director of the visual culture museum M+, adds oil to the revolving door that is senior management of West Kowloon Cultural District. It reminds us of the inability of West Kowloon Cultural District Authority to retain vastly overpriced imported personnel.

Had the Cultural District been a listed company, this merry-go-round of instability would see its shares nosedive as investors flee, yet the Authority simply starts another expensive global search for a replacement. Why does it do this?

The investors in this arts hub are the people of Hong Kong, and we deserve better than the shenanigans dealt to us thus far. It is an internationally recognised joke. Delays and vast cost overruns show our city as unable to build the world-class infrastructures required, while other cities in China and Asia deliver stunning cultural centres.

The Cultural District Authority must stop the loss of senior staff and explore fully the filling of these positions with local talent, people who see life in Hong Kong as more than a five-year well-paid posting. I wonder how many Hong Kong communities actually know the names of departed (and departing) senior cultural district personnel Graham Sheffield, Michael Lynch, Tobias Berger or Nittve; I hazard not many.

The Cultural District needs stability that can only come from hiring people committed to their future in Hong Kong as part of the fabric of our city.

It should not simply import another person with scant regard for the community of Hong Kong.

Mark Peaker, The Peak

Catholic clerics sent divisive message

As the world celebrates its maturity by recognising the rights of the lesbian, gay, bisexual and transgender (LGBT) community, it is ironic that Hong Kong's two leading Catholics, Cardinal John Tong Hon and his Auxiliary Bishop, Michael Yeung Ming-cheung, show a lack of maturity and prejudice against the LGBT community.

To compare humans who seek no more than to share their life with a person they love to that of a drug abuser is repugnant and reflects the divisive and naive nature of the bishop.

To pressure voters to consider the sexuality of a candidate in the district council elections is bemusing given the long history of closeted homosexuality in the Catholic Church.

That Cardinal Tong wishes to impose his biased views on his followers does nothing but divide people.

The Catholic Church is in no position to judge.

Hopefully, the ignorance of these two clerics will be disregarded by a public far more enlightened than those who, rather than preach inclusion and acceptance, the core values of Christianity, choose to create a divisive atmosphere. They should both be ashamed.

Mark Peaker, The Peak

Clueless culture chiefs are no surprise

It should come as no shock that the tenants of PMQ are considering a "mass exodus" as they vent their frustrations on a management wholly unsuited to the development of a cultural hub ("Tenants unhappy amid exodus worries", November 19).

We need only look at our hapless government's other ventures to see how clueless and devoid of cultural imagination and creativity those appointed are. As PMQ becomes just another soulless building, we can await with despair the opening of Central Police Station, which has more hope of incarcerating culture than developing it for Hong Kong.

Mark Peaker, The Peak

Taxpayer loses out again to MTR Corp

The embarrassment of the MTR Corporation and its failure to deliver on time and within budget the high-speed rail link to the mainland ("Bailout for MTR's high-speed rail line", December 1) reflects Hong Kong's declining ability as a city that was once proud of its achievements.

Yet more laughable is the comment by MTR Corp chairman, Dr Raymond Chien Kuo-fung, as he states his company is "financially sound with capital reserves of HK$68 billion".

Perhaps he has not heard of the term "withdrawal" and sees nothing wrong with the MTR Corp robbing the Hong Kong taxpayer of an additional HK$19.6 billion as he praises the supposed excellent fiscal management of the MTR Corp.

Mark Peaker, The Peak

A poor record by most measures

Mok Wai-chuen's defence of the Environmental Protection Department's competence in battling our declining air quality is laughable. He states that from "mid-December 2011 to the end of October 2015, law enforcement officers timed 4,712 vehicles with idling engines and issued fixed penalty tickets to 186 drivers who violated the ordinance"; this equates to about four tickets per month. Is this a result to be proud of?

The lethargic attitude of the department and traffic wardens is reprehensible and requires a strategic rethink of the ridiculous Strategic Traffic Enforcement Policy, which was established in 1993 with a primary aim of the "maintenance of smooth traffic flows" but has simply allowed police to avoid dealing with the plethora of illegally parked cars that on a daily basis block our roads.

That he concludes by stating "drivers are now generally more mindful of switching off idling engines than before" clearly reflects his department's utter ignorance of the continuous abuse of the idling law on virtually every street in Hong Kong.

Mark Peaker, The Peak

2016

Only thing lacking is political will

Turning Professor Nelson Chow Wing-sun's research report into policy is indeed a different matter, as Chief Secretary Carrie Lam Cheng Yuet-ngor rightly stated ("War of words: Carrie Lam says Hong Kong government adviser on retirement protection doesn't fully understand public financing", December 23). It is, however, an easy one, for it requires nothing more than a willingness from our government to honour the commitment our elderly have made in the creation of Hong Kong.

For a city that has no issue funding bridges that no one asked for, or bailing out profit-making organisations that fail to meet budgets, or cultural centres which vacuum up funds with scant regard to delivering the promised product, there should be no delay in delivering to our elderly their right to enjoy their old age with dignity and grace.

Age will not weary them, nor the years condemn but our government just might!

Mark Peaker, The Peak

Zero tolerance on abuse of disabled bays

I refer to Gordon Loch's letter regarding able-bodied drivers using disabled bays ("Misuse of parking space for disabled", January 4). It is the ultimate in arrogance when this happens. There should be zero tolerance on this issue.

In the Pacific Place car park, it is often abused and I have no qualms in positioning the movable disabled sign right beside the driver's door to remind the selfish person of their thoughtless behaviour.

This, however, is mild when compared to an incident I observed last year in London. A disabled car driver was incandescent with rage when an able-bodied person refused to move their car to allow him to park and unload his disabled daughter; after a terse exchange of words, the driver of the disabled vehicle picked up a metal chair from an outside cafe and smashed it through the windscreen of the able-bodied person's car.

Perhaps that was not the correct course of action but one completely understandable to any of us who have to deal with people who park in disabled bays.

Mark Peaker, The Peak

Time to change the cast and script

Listening to Sarah Palin endorse Donald Trump as America's next president should be relegated to a B-grade afternoon movie. To hear her announce that "this is gonna be so much fun" reflects the complete lack of awareness she has for the fragile state of the world; that she and Donald Trump and their bigoted right-wing views create hatred and division should be part of a poorly written script.

Yet, even Hollywood seems to understand the role of the presidency better; in Michael Douglas' 1995 film *The American President*, his character makes a speech far more compelling than the drivel we hear from Trump.

Douglas' character declares "America isn't easy. America is advanced citizenship. You gotta want it bad, 'cause it's gonna put up a fight. It's gonna say, 'You want free speech? Let's see you acknowledge a man whose words make your blood boil, who's standing centre stage and advocating at the top of his lungs that which you would spend a lifetime opposing at the top of yours. You want to claim this land as the land of the free? Then the symbol of your country can't just be a flag; it also has to be one of its citizens exercising his right to burn that flag in protest'."

Perhaps we need another actor to be president?

Mark Peaker, The Peak

02/03/2016

Vote yes to ensure the UK remains dominant power in Europe

In response to Jerry Wraith's letter ("Register so you can vote for British EU exit", February 27) reminding all eligible persons to register in order for them to vote the United Kingdom "out" in the pending referendum on European Union membership, I agree, but register to vote and keep the UK "in".

Mr Wraith talks of the "eventual disappearance" of the UK as a country. What folly drives him to make such a comment lies at the foundation of the scaremongering of those who seek to destroy a union that has allowed Europe to enjoy

unprecedented decades of peace and prosperity, free from the individual pursuits of the old empires that twice drove Europe to war.

Membership of the EU is a privilege, yet like membership to any prestigious club, one at times has to deal with irritating fellow members and be governed by rules that do not always make sense.

Yet, to resign membership will often see a former member regret their decision and earnestly seek a way back in. This is the reality for Britain should it seek to leave the EU.

The EU clearly needs reform, but that can only be achieved by being a member.

The emotive rhetoric of the "out" supporters are reactions to the state of the EU today. However, they give no indication to a future European community that has every chance to develop into the greatest alliance of economic power the world has ever seen.

To not be a part of this is lunacy and will result in a UK begging for scraps from a union it was once at the core of.

I agree with Mr Wraith that all of us who are eligible to vote do, but vote to remain in and ensure that our UK remains a dominant power within the EU.

Mark Peaker, The Peak

What is CY angling for with new idea?

It is abhorrent that Chief Executive Leung Chun-ying refers to the "working class" in his puerile idea to create three lunchtime angling zones and a swimming shed for the masses to enjoy "after a simple lunch" ("Get reel, CY: angling zone plan ridiculed", March 9).

Perhaps I am mistaken but Mr Leung is not of noble birth and earns his crust as an employee of the state. He is, by simple definition, working class.

There is a cut-off between working class and middle class, one having discretionary income, rather than simply sustenance. Do we conclude that our chief executive hopes his working-class people can also fish for their supper?

Mark Peaker, The Peak

Grappa's just another mall restaurant

In his letter "Swire should allow Grappa's to stay open" (April 2), Mark Hill beseeches Swire to allow Grappa's to remain in Pacific Place mall.

He compares the eatery to true Hong Kong landmarks such as the Noonday Gun, Peak Tram and the Hong Kong Club.

Such a comparison is foolhardy, for the Noonday Gun dates back to 1860, its daily firing the result of a penalty imposed on Jardines by a senior British naval officer. The Peak Tram started operating in 1888 and was a remarkable piece of engineering that now carries more than four million people annually, or an average of over 11,000 every day. The Hong Kong Club was the first gentlemen's club in Hong Kong and opened on May 26, 1846.

These are core parts of Hong Kong's heritage that survive to this day and continue to be a part of the fabric of our society; they have seen war and bewildering changes and have each, in their own way, adapted to their ever-changing surroundings. Grappa's, I am afraid, does not meet the exalted status Mr Hill feels it deserves; a restaurant in a shopping mall, regardless of its longevity, must also adapt.

Swire offered Grappa's an opportunity to evolve and continue but this was not accepted. Swire's aim was to ensure Grappa's remained, the decision to leave was made by El Grande Concepts.

Mark Peaker, The Peak

01/05/2016

LGBT equality must be a priority

The opportunity for Hong Kong to host the Gay Games is a chance for the lesbian, gay, bisexual and transgender (LGBT) community to show that being homosexual is to be normal ("Hong Kong to propose hosting the gay Olympics", April 24).

In a city where same-sex relationships remain unrecognised by a government that fails to understand that inclusion and participation are core values of a mature society, the Gay Games allows an understanding of diversity to be presented through sport, where it is not your sexual orientation but rather your ability that matters. It will also allow those who perceive the homosexual and transgender community as one defined purely along sexual desire to understand that being LGBT is to be a part of the fabric of every community in Hong Kong.

Founded in 1994 to coincide with the 25th anniversary of the Stonewall Riots, arguably the start of the modern LGBT movement, the Games have become a beacon of inclusion and tolerance; two values Hong Kong has in recent years lost.

I hope Hong Kong wins, but if it does not, to have been selected should remind our government that to be a world-class city, we need world-class values, and the recognition of same-sex marriages and the acknowledgement that the LGBT community is equal must ensue.

Mark Peaker, The Peak

Councillor was aiming at wrong target

Central and Western District councillor Ted Hui Chi-fung seeks to create recognition for himself with the unfortunate collapse of a partial part of a building within the Central Police Station renovation area.

Describing the incident as "an international joke" is absurd. The rest of the world is not monitoring Hong Kong's building renovation.

Yet any international visitor will leave the city with abundant memories of illegally parked cars clogging our streets and pavements, and rightly condemn Hong Kong as an international joke – streets that mostly fall within the jurisdiction of the Central and Western District and illegality it does nothing to curtail.

Mark Peaker, The Peak

Those who seek to oppress will not win

The tragedy that has befallen Orlando, Florida, is heart-wrenching; the loss of life unbearable for those who are left to mourn.

The callous feebleness of the person driven to such an act by the vile pursuit of an ideology founded upon hatred has gained no ground in its doomed path for dominance.

In targeting the lesbian, gay, bisexual and transgender (LGBT) community, of which I am part, they have merely strengthened our resolve.

Those who seek to oppress will not succeed, for humanity is stronger.

Our community is unfairly referred to as one of "sexual orientation"; sex is not the foundation of our lives. The LGBT community strives for love, friendship and long-term commitment just as non-same-sex couples desire.

We are your pilots, your soldiers, your brothers and sisters, we are you and we are one, united in our resilience against any brotherhood of hate. May those who lost their lives in Orlando, Florida, rest in peace. Your deaths will always be remembered.

Mark Peaker, The Peak

We have had enough of bad taxi drivers

Chau Kwok-keung, spokesman for the Anti-Taxi Franchises Concern Group, bemoans that the prospect of a premium taxi service is unfair to them ("Taxi siege set to drive home message against franchises", June 21).

Perhaps he might wish to be reminded that for years Hong Kong citizens have had to endure a taxi service that has been wholly unfair to us.

We have to put up with filthy taxis and obnoxious drivers who smoke inside their vehicles, drive with scant regard to safety, have dashboards resembling the bridge of the Starship Enterprise, overcharge and refuse fares that don't suit them.

I doubt many people in Hong Kong will feel any pity for a taxi service that has become one of the worst in Asia.

The arrival of Uber demonstrated that a decent service still exists in our city, but you require decent people to run it. Our taxi drivers are simply not up to the quality Asia's world city demands.

Mark Peaker, The Peak

28/06/2016

Time to step up building inspections

The tragic loss of the lives of two firemen highlights the woeful inadequacy of the Buildings Department and its failure to ensure safety regulations are implemented and adhered to. One only has to walk the internal staircases of virtually any building in Hong Kong to see them obstructed with debris; the recent trend for "mini-storage" has seen warehouses carved up with scant regard for regulations on what is placed within them – there are no checks to see if items stored are inflammable or toxic.

The Buildings Department has failed completely in its own Mandatory Building Inspection Scheme, and, as a result, we have two firefighters dead.

The government is to blame; it does not insist that smoke detectors are installed in all buildings. Safety is always second to profit and this must stop.

Mark Peaker, The Peak

11/07/2016

Parents should not depend on lifeguards

The furore over swimming pool safety at a Discovery Bay [Recreation] Club mirrors a culture of blaming others for one's own mistake.

Lifeguards never guarantee safety and they cannot save everyone; they are a precautionary measure to safeguard those who cannot save themselves.

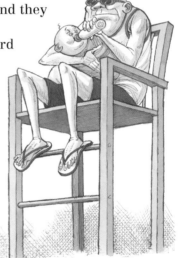

When I was a boy, we were commanded by parents to "stay within sight" and constantly observed, not by strangers but by family. The primary responsibility for a child's safety in the water is with the person charged to look after them, to monitor them, to ensure they can swim within their capabilities and to never let that child out of their sight.

Parents should not relegate this role to a person employed to oversee safety in an overcrowded pool.

Mark Peaker, The Peak

Food trucks show city's true spirit

How refreshing to see Hong Kong's entrepreneurial spirit alive and well with the competitive flair deployed to win the first phase of the food truck allocation ("Victory tastes good: 16 winners of food truck cook-off selected after heated competition", July 27). It is a reminder that away from the negative actions of those who seek to divide Hong Kong along political lines, we remain at heart a city capable of tremendous originality and ability.

Now let's just hope the trucks will not be parked on double yellow lines.

Mark Peaker, The Peak

So far, zombie annoyance not off the scale

As Pokemon Go hit Hong Kong, I was expecting a whirlwind of zombies aimlessly walking around knocking into me as they failed to look where they are walking.

I have been pleasantly surprised that for the most part this has not happened, save for one direct hit in the IFC [International Finance Centre] mall over the weekend, to which the offender was profusely apologetic.

Perhaps our Pokemon Go players can be rated like our typhoons – P1 for slightly annoying, P3 for bumping into you, but without intent, P8 for a jolt and P10 for full-force collision that requires verbal interaction.

Mark Peaker, The Peak

Sentences for student leaders too lenient

How pathetic that magistrate June Cheung Tin-ngan has handed down such lenient sentences to Nathan Law Kwun-chung, Joshua Wong Chi-fung and Alex Chow Yong-kang ("No jail for Occupy leaders Joshua Wong and Nathan Law, with Law still clear for Legco run", August 15).

That these three are free to pursue their academic and other careers because the magistrate described them as passionate and genuinely believing of their political ideals reeks of a decision based on personal bias and not the rule of law. Occupy Central held our city to ransom for 79 days. Hong Kong does not belong to these hooligans or their comrades who campaign with hate and violence.

The smug faces of the three as they exited the court reflects the contempt in which they hold the law and the citizens of Hong Kong.

Mark Peaker, The Peak

City's airline has been dealt unfair hand

Cathay Pacific's 82 per cent decline in first-half net profit is understandably disappointing.

Competition and economics deal our adopted city flagbearer an unfair hand when it is forced to compete against government-subsidised airlines or those which operate from a substantially lower cost base.

Yet Cathay strives to continually offer levels of service, professionalism and, above all, safety that other airlines do not.

Cathay's investment in the latest aircraft, the A350-900, reflects the company's quest for superiority. The interior is fitted out with the latest in-flight entertainment systems, Wi-Fi connection, superior seat comfort in all three classes, and an aircraft at the forefront of environmental concerns and quietness.

Customers have a plethora of choices when choosing to fly and Cathay recognises this.

As an airline that has served as an emblem of Hong Kong for decades, I am confident that the overall excellence of Cathay Pacific will see it through this present patch of turbulence.

Mark Peaker, The Peak

10/09/2016

Lawmakers should focus on dialogue

The record voter turnout for the Legco election is a good thing, regardless of one's personal political persuasion.

One hopes that this chamber will use dialogue, discussion, debate and logic for the betterment of all Hong Kong and we shall see an end to elected members who have placed their own agenda and vanity over that of the people they represent.

We need never forget that Hong Kong is a diverse city with a depth of talent that needs to be nurtured and developed. It is a long-haul obligation to serve, not a short-term opportunity for self-gratification.

Mark Peaker, The Peak

Camera tickets good way to deter offenders

The release of the Transport Complaints Unit quarterly report and its revelation that illegal parking is a problem in Hong Kong is welcome.

Illegal parking is rampant and thus far the relevant authorities have shown a grossly inadequate response to enforcing existing laws, thus creating a culture of arrogance among drivers and self-righteous belief that they can park anywhere.

Police bear a large amount of the blame for the abuse of the law, either ignoring illegally parked cars or simply ushering them away to allow them to drive around the block and park back in the same spot.

Traffic wardens are a rarer breed than most endangered species and are seldom to be seen, let alone actually writing a ticket.

Given the ineffectual capabilities of our uniformed law enforcers, it is time for camera enforcement that automatically tickets offending vehicles. This system has seen a dramatic improvement in efforts to curb illegal parking in European cities. Asia's world city deserves more than the car park the government's ridiculous selective traffic enforcement programme has allowed it to become.

Mark Peaker, The Peak

Criticism of Cathay Pacific is very unfair

Henry Ng appears to find no comfort in Cathay Pacific, and his letter expressed his disdain for the airline ("Cathay needs to think less about savings and more about customers", October 13).

He is certainly entitled to his view, but constructive criticism cannot be so lopsided. Cathay Pacific has become an easy target for disgruntled passengers who seem to feel the airline fails to deliver. However, this is not true.

Cathay has invested significantly in product development, which is most visible with the arrival of the latest A350 aircraft, with newly styled interiors in all three classes that ensure passenger comfort and safety.

Cathay lounges around the world offer a superlative experience before departure and upon arrival in certain destinations. Cathay is a commercial entity; it needs to make a profit and strives to do so without government subsidies that benefit many Middle Eastern and some Asian carriers. Mr Ng comments that "passengers are lucky if they don't get frowned on by a member of staff" – what nonsense. Cathay staff are professional, polite and courteous but subjected often to unruly behaviour that may indeed warrant being frowned upon.

The present furore about adding an additional seat is understandable, but the new design of the seats will continue to match, and in many cases surpass, that offered by other airlines which offer a less complete service.

The wording used by CEO Ivan Chu Kwok-leung was perhaps clumsy but reflects merely his desire to ensure Cathay remains a leading carrier.

Cathay Pacific knows that passengers have choices and for 70 years has been an integral part of the success of Hong Kong. It is an achievement that Swire is proud of and one that will continue.

Mark Peaker, The Peak

Puerile antics have no place in legislature

The puerile antics of Younspiration lawmakers Sixtus Baggio Leung Chung-hang and Yau Wai-ching reflect their own vanity in seeking to place themselves above the people of Hong Kong. It has been heart-warming to see the backlash from people they naively thought would support them. Their antics and foul-mouthed behaviour do not reflect Hong Kong or the majority of the people in this city.

The Legislative Council, regardless of one's political persuasion, remains our city's centre of government, and the swearing of an oath is a solemn process that demands respect.

Calls for an independent Hong Kong are futile – the rest of the world recognises Hong Kong as part of China, this is not going to change. It is time for Hong Kong to focus on the inadequacies of our own government and fix the many parts of our city that are broken.

We waste time on these fools as the hungry go unfed, the poor forgotten, our hospitals overflow and our roads clogged by arrogant drivers who, like many Legco members, consider themselves above the law.

Hong Kong has real problems; it is time to focus on our city and leave the shenanigans of self-importance behind.

Mark Peaker, The Peak

Is democracy all it's cracked up to be?

I refer to Shirley Lee's letter ("Trump, Brexit raise doubts on voting system", November 18).

Ms Lee is seemingly confused when she states that "virtually everyone had been predicting a win for Hillary Clinton". Had she spoken to Donald Trump supporters, they most assuredly were not "taken by surprise". The same can be said of the 52 per cent of Britons who voted for Brexit in the EU referendum.

The entire foundation of democracy is that we elect a person the people vote for (albeit Clinton won the popular vote but was not elected, that is a flaw of the American system).

There is no requirement for previous experience, no requirement for suitability and no requirement to implement the policy ideals that may get a person elected.

The shocked reaction to Trump and Brexit is simply because Ms Lee and millions of others are on the losing side – too bad, that's democracy. Her argument for Hong Kong is pointless, we are not a democracy and based upon her own argument, perhaps democracy isn't all it's cracked up to be.

Mark Peaker, The Peak

Patronising Patten just a relic of empire

The Last Governor should be the title of a film starring Hollywood A-list actors, instead it is the frequent repeat of a B-list politician and a Z-list diplomat.

That Chris Patten descends into Hong Kong to lord it over his former flock is bad enough. That he finds it his role to tell those who held our city to ransom for 79 days that they were the "brave young people of Hong Kong who established the moral high ground about democracy" is patronising in the extreme, coming from a man imposed on the city without any democratic process whatsoever.

Had he been one iota more diligent in his role in crafting the wording that defined Hong Kong's return to China, perhaps we wouldn't be in the pickle we now find ourselves.

Patten sailed away from Hong Kong wrapped in the privilege of his suite aboard *Britannia*; like the ship itself, he should now be retired and seen as nothing more relevant than a faded part of empire.

Mark Peaker, The Peak

2017

Consultation on museum not necessary

The decision to build a branch of the Palace Museum in Hong Kong should be received with gratitude.

The West Kowloon Cultural District has failed to deliver any of its proposed artistic and cultural benefits to the city, and for former chief executive Michael Lynch to express shock that the Hong Kong public were not consulted is hypocritical. Were we consulted when he was appointed at vast cost to the public purse?

Those who claim it further undermines Hong Kong's autonomy are wrong.

The public does not need to be consulted on every issue and certainly not one that brings benefit to our waning tourist industry and employment to many.

When the museum opens, the people of Hong Kong will flock to it, to see the magnificence of China's history, its art and its culture.

They will be reminded of a country that Hong Kong has always been, and will forever remain, a part of.

Mark Peaker, The Peak

Thatcher took a broken UK and fixed it

Paul Serfaty is wrong with his negative comparison of Carrie Lam Cheng Yuet-ngor and Margaret Thatcher ("Lam must not emulate later era Thatcher", January 17).

Thatcher took a broken Britain and fixed it. She destroyed the stranglehold of the unions over British industry, made Britain competitive within Europe and around the world, and she remains our greatest post-war leader.

If Carrie Lam or John Tsang Chun-wah governs Hong Kong with the passion with which Thatcher led Britain, we will see a resurgent city, free of the self-righteous importance of the few, replaced with the determined direction of the many.

Mark Peaker, The Peak

Thatcher was praised by rivals as well

Keith McNab ("City does not need divisive Thatcher clone", February 3) says that my "outlandish statement" in my letter ("Thatcher took a broken UK and fixed it", January 20) "cannot go unanswered". Neither can his inability to accept the reality of Margaret Thatcher.

She transformed Britain in a way few other prime ministers before or since have done. As an impatient reformer, she set about deconstructing Britain's almost Eastern European state-dominated economy.

Trades union barons were put to the sword, taxes cut and people empowered to own their own homes. It was a social revolution, the like of which has rarely been seen, and which endures to this day.

Instead of a brain drain, Britain got an influx of talent and money, drawn by our low-tax, high-enterprise economy.

Ex-deputy leader of the Labour Party Roy Hattersley described Thatcher as "one of the two greatest prime ministers of the 20th century". Perhaps Thatcher's greatest reform was the Labour Party where Tony Blair had to pay tribute to her legacy before the British people would elect him.

Politics is the ability to have views, hold to them and drive them through to success.

Should Carrie Lam Cheng Yuet-ngor or John Tsang Chun-wah have half of Thatcher's skill, then Hong Kong will be resurgent.

Mark Peaker, The Peak

Next leader must respect LGBT rights

The issue of lesbian, gay, bisexual, transgender (LGBT) rights is not a core concern for any of the chief executive candidates.

Carrie Lam Cheng Yuet-ngor's perceived hypocrisy ("Lam angers both sides in same-sex marriage", February 16) is founded in her ignorance of the issue, coupled with her own religious beliefs. Should she become chief executive, she will need to understand the values that the LGBT population living in Hong Kong add to the fabric of our society and comprehend how not being an LGBT-tolerant society diminishes our international reputation and economic prowess.

No chief executive can avoid the issue of developing Hong Kong into a world-class society that is inclusive for all its citizens. Roger Wong Wai-ming, convenor of the Family School Sexual Orientation Discrimination Ordinance Concern

Group, is wholly flawed in his logic that a more tolerant society weakens traditional family values. It strengthens them, it allows all members of a family to be honest. Since when has honesty been a betrayal of conscience?

The facts speak for themselves. In the past 15 years, the acceptance of LGBT by those aged between 18 and 32 has grown from 51 per cent in 2003 to 70 per cent in 2016. These young people, born since 1980, are the future of our society and, unlike members of Roger Wong's concern group, represent a future based on education, understanding, tolerance and humanity.

Hong Kong claims to be Asia's world city, so our next chief executive must embrace diversity as we seek to unite our city into a place where the aspirations of all are treated equally.

Mark Peaker, The Peak

Gay Games bid a moment of pride for HK

Congratulations to Dennis Philipse and his team for their hard work in getting Hong Kong shortlisted for the 2022 Gay Games.

Our three chief executive candidates must now voice their support for this world-class event which brings international recognition, prosperity and tolerance.

As Asia's perceived world city, it is time for our government to recognise that by accepting diversity, we strengthen the values of society as a whole.

Hong Kong is being presented with an opportunity to show the world how great we can be; let's all work together to ensure this moment is not lost to homophobic ignorance.

Mark Peaker, The Peak

Cowardly terrorists will never succeed

The tragedy that struck Westminster Bridge in London on Wednesday reminds us again of the frailty of our peace and that those who seek to undermine our way of life will never succeed.

Those who choose to kill innocent people reveal only their own cowardice and failures. Christian, Muslim, Jew, Buddhist, we are the foundation of humanity, and no individual who kills in God's name shall ever win.

Mark Peaker, The Peak

No "time warp" as Cathay soars in excellence

Peter Guy's assault on Cathay Pacific ("A flawed business model in a changing world", March 26) reflects more his outdated views of the airline industry than Cathay being "in a time warp".

Cathay continues to deliver the newest aircraft with the latest technology to benefit both passengers and the environment; it strives to deliver state-of-the-art products that benefit passengers, by allowing them to remain connected throughout a flight on the new A350 aircraft; it envelops passengers in the Cathay product from check-in to arrival, with a lounge system that is unsurpassed in terms of amenities and convenience.

Peter Guy glosses over the fact that Cathay is one of the world's safest airlines and, for this, many passengers accept a premium on fares that are already competitively priced.

His rant about passengers paying for the third runway is factually inaccurate, as are his uninformed views on Cathay's profitability. As part of the Swire family, the Cathay Pacific product remains an integral component of a company that remains committed to the excellence of service it has prided itself on for generations. There is no time warp at Cathay, unless one sees in this benchmark airline the future of flying.

Mark Peaker, The Peak

Do not ignore terror threat from vehicles

Hong Kong is a target for terrorism, that is a given ("Police on alert for lone wolf terrorism", May 4). But are our police diligent in their detection of potential threats? That is an unknown.

When the Irish Republic Army was terrorising London, bombs placed in illegally parked cars was a common tactic. Both the Harrods [1983] and Hyde Park [1982] bombs were hidden in vehicles.

The apathy with which our police handle illegal parking in Hong Kong creates a dangerous precedent for allowing such threats to exist here.

Vigilance is essential for the effective enforcement of all our laws, not ignoring a threat, wherever it may occur.

Mark Peaker, The Peak

27/05/2017

Great flying experience second to none

Cathay Pacific is striving to offer what you call for in your editorial ("Cathay needs to focus on delivering that 'great flight experience'", May 23).

I was recently transferred to a British Airways [BA] flight from London to Hong Kong as my Cathay flight was cancelled. Having horrid memories of BA, I had some trepidation but thought it would be the new A380 with the all-new first-class product. It was an equally new 777/300 and it was horrendous. Cathay has six suites for first class where BA has 20 semi-private seats that are inferior to Cathay's new A350 business-class seat. The cabin floor was littered with debris, and the service, while pleasant, was not a patch on Cathay.

Cathay is Hong Kong's airline and those who keep knocking it should be reminded how lucky we are to have one that sits at the forefront of safety and service. The present restructuring is a result of past errors. Job losses are unfortunate but, at times, necessary to ensure a brand that defines the excellence of Hong Kong survives.

Cathay offers outstanding service, and its continual service improvements create a flying experience that is second to none across all classes.

Mark Peaker, The Peak

28/06/2017

City remains one of freest economies

It was to be expected that activist Joshua Wong Chi-fung and his fellow disillusioned foot soldiers would reappear as the territory celebrates 20 years of success following the end of the colonial era ("Activists target bauhinia statue ahead of Xi visit", June 27).

Hong Kong remains one of the world's freest economies; a place where if you meet this city half way and are prepared to work, it will reward you. Joshua Wong fails in his puerile attacks because he does not understand that Hong Kong is loved by most of the people who live here.

We are not looking for a divorce with Beijing.

Recent comments from former leaders that we need to embrace China, and understand that to work with China offers only betterment for all the citizens of Hong Kong, is something these activists cannot comprehend. This is because competition to succeed requires more than a whining insistence that life is so hard.

I salute Hong Kong for the past 20 years and look forward to the next exciting 20; Hong Kong – the best city in China.

Mark Peaker, The Peak

See high-speed railway as an opportunity

For those who harp on about immigration checks for the new rail terminus, let us remember the bigger picture.

Railways create opportunities. They were critical to the industrial revolution and the development of European economies, and they remain vitally relevant today.

The linking of Hong Kong to the rest of China via high-speed rail networks gives access and opportunity for those who realise the importance of China's growing economy.

We should be thankful to have such unhindered access to it.

Mark Peaker, The Peak

Original punishment was too lenient

The international press has a jaundiced view of Hong Kong.

The imprisonment of Joshua Wong, Nathan Law and Alex Chow is not "the latest sign of Beijing's clampdown on dissent" as the *Financial Times* claimed.

The public outcry by the vast majority of Hong Kong people in reaction to the ridiculously lenient sentences originally handed down was echoed by the courts.

They used the judicial appeal system to legally re-examine the facts and hand down sentences that reflected the violent acts these three perpetuated and encouraged others to do.

There has been no "transparent attempt under pressure from Beijing", simply the use of our courts to fit the punishment to the crime. Hong Kong remains a city where the rule of law prevails, independently.

Mark Peaker, The Peak

Aghast at lack of action over illegal land use

The Lands Department's appalling record of enforcement is reprehensible ("No action taken for 20 years over illegal land use", September 13).

That a spokesman has the audacity to state they deal with "straightforward cases first, and thorny cases last" is laughable.

Perhaps all those with illegal structures need only grow a rose garden to evade prosecution.

Mark Peaker, The Peak

Intolerance will not end with Games

Luisa Tam condemns the government's lukewarm reaction to the city winning the Gay Games bid for 2022 ("Government shows true colours with its response to Gay Games", November 7). As a gay man and initially asked to be involved with this bid, let me frankly respond to her comments.

The bid was never supported by any government officials. They neither provided support nor sought to dissuade, they remained neutral. That the bid is successful is good but, to be blunt, it is not something that the majority of Hong Kong citizens are particularly focused on.

The city faces several issues right now and 2022 is deemed too far away. A sporting event, gay or otherwise, is not a priority. Discrimination will exist before, during and after the games.

Those who argue that for the lesbian, gay, bisexual and transgender (LGBT) community to demand acceptance and tolerance and then request the opposite by hosting an event deemed exclusively for them (yes, we know the games are open to all sexual orientations), only confuse the issue.

Tolerance of alternate lifestyles can never be won if it is placed on a pedestal of egoism.

The government has "noted" the win, and I am confident it will seek to liaise with the relevant people to ensure that by 2022 the city will be ready to proudly host an international event that reflects the open-mindedness of Hong Kong.

The success in winning this bid should be used as an avenue of communication with the majority of Hong Kong people who still question a lifestyle they remain ignorant of.

Winning the bid was the easy step; educating the city that tolerance of diversity isn't just for an event in 2022 but a journey for life is what is now required.

Mark Peaker, The Peak

Illegal parking is also linked to littering

The recent focus on plastic debris desecrating our oceans is oddly enough linked to Hong Kong's inability to tackle illegal parking.

Drivers who sit in their parked vehicles for hours often eat from polystyrene boxes wrapped in plastic bags. When the meal is finished, they bizarrely tie the bag up neatly then toss it out the window into the street.

Our city's charmless taxi drivers feel this is their right, and any early morning walk around Hong Kong streets will see the kerbside littered with such debris, most of which ends up in our harbour.

Our police are lethargic in their tackling of illegal parking, but perhaps a desire to see our own beaches free from litter may prompt them to be a little more assertive with illegal parking and illegal littering.

Mark Peaker, The Peak

2018

Brexit UK can hardly afford to irk Beijing

Living in Hong Kong, one can still see relics of empire, manufactured items that were delivered to the colonies despite an ability for local companies to produce them.

As British leader Theresa May travels across China, she no longer represents a country that produces much at all, a fact that Brexiteers fail to recognise, as they seek the halcyon memories of empire.

China's Belt and Road Initiative is indeed a resurgence of the Middle Kingdom to dominate global trade and, as the British Empire did, benefit itself while offering economic advantage to those it works with.

The United Kingdom would do well not to irk the Middle Kingdom too much. As the Brexit day of March 29, 2019 – the date for the UK to leave the European Union – draws closer, we really cannot be too fussy about who we seek to trade with.

Mark Peaker, The Peak

Keeping right on new bridge not so simple

Transport sector lawmaker Frankie Yick Chi-ming expects drivers to take no time adapting to driving on "the other side of the road" ("Right side of road the only way to travel on Hong Kong-Zhuhai-Macau bridge", February 13).

He said "many occasional drivers have also driven overseas, such as in Europe and the US. Switching sides should be a breeze".

What Mr Yick fundamentally fails to comprehend is that these drivers hire cars designed to be driven on the right, where the golden rule of the driver being closest to the road centre is easily managed.

Driving a left-hand car on the right, or vice versa, where the driving position places one kerbside, leads to confusion, or worse.

Mark Peaker, The Peak

Cathay never stops in quest for the best

I refer to the article on Cathay by Peter Guy ("Cathay Pacific is a case study in how most companies fail in the long run, if they don't change", March 11).

To opine that Cathay Pacific does not evolve reflects ignorance of the steps Cathay Pacific continually undertakes to ensure that its aircraft, the technology on board and on the ground continue to deliver a customer experience that remains among the best.

It cannot be assumed that all passengers desire are cheap seats, claiming that "new competitive dynamics have sucked in all airlines whether they like it or not".

One only has to look at the decline of British Airways to see how an airline that lets go of its brand integrity and service is destined for failure.

Cathay Pacific pursues a course of not becoming a budget airline because a vast number of clients enjoy full-service providers with an assurance of quality and safety that others fail to invest in.

Swire retains long-term employees because of the excellence of the company and a proven commitment to reward merit with promotion. Loyalty may be old-fashioned but remains superior to the "ruthless innovation and decision making" that short-term opportunistic business decisions offer. Cathay Pacific is here for the long haul and shall continue to offer excellence of product across all its travel classes.

Mark Peaker, The Peak

Crackdown on careless driving fails road test

It seems Martin Cadman, chief superintendent of the police's traffic branch, isn't clearly relaying his message to subordinates ("'Every uniformed officer' to join Hong Kong police crackdown on careless driving", March 29).

Cadman said that "this operation will be conducted not just by traffic police officers, but by all uniformed police officers throughout Hong Kong. They will do it on foot and in vehicles. They will use personal observation and traffic enforcement equipment".

On April 16, while waiting to cross Jackson Road, I saw five officers on the opposite side. As the lights on Chater Road turned red, two vehicles drove through, turning right onto Jackson Road. It was clear to everyone who had to wait despite having a green walk light. The group of five officers, who could not have failed to see the offence, did nothing. I stopped and questioned the senior officer. He initially feigned ignorance, then said it was "not their job".

Mark Peaker, The Peak

Cutting corners can't be par for the course

Jason Wong-Chi-ching, general manager of the Sha Tin-Central rail link project, is fundamentally wrong if he accepts that cost-cutting is "normal procedure on-site that happens every day" ("Hong Kong's Sha Tin-Central rail link hit by corner-cutting contractor's shoddy work on platforms, MTR Corp confirms", May 31). His complacency raises the worry of just how many other inappropriate steps have been taken that place the future safety of passengers at risk?

Mark Peaker, The Peak

Are we to start stoning homosexuals next?

The decision of the Court of Appeal to overturn a landmark decision to establish Hong Kong as a fair, tolerant and inclusive society shames our city ("Ruling a setback for Hong Kong's image as a fair and tolerant city", June 3).

The rest of the world is recognising same-sex marriage as a basic human right, yet Asia's laughably self-styled "world city" fails to do so.

The appeal court justices hide conveniently behind the letter of the city's mini-constitution, failing to take into consideration the groundswell of support for LGBT rights in our city and showing Hong Kong to be a backward culture where archaic interpretations of marriage, based on outdated religious doctrine, prevail. Are we to start stoning homosexuals next?

As a gay person, I am disgusted by this ruling and our government's failure to recognise that equality is a basic human right to be shared by all, regardless of colour, national origin, religion, gender or sexual orientation.

Mark Peaker, The Peak

Hong Kong has a long way to go on LGBT rights

The change of sentiment among most Hongkongers towards the LGBT community is pleasing.

Yet, as long as we have a government that feels as though it is their place to indoctrinate their interpretation of marriage and equality, little will change in our city ("Study shows growing support for same-sex marriage in Hong Kong", July 3).

Gigi Chao, daughter of tycoon Cecil Chao Sze-tsung, is correct in saying that the long-standing stigma against homosexuals won't go away unless people are more open about discussing sexual diversity. However, Ms Chao left out one word – people have to "accept" sexual diversity and recognise that it is not sexual depravity.

We need large local employers to understand and implement policies that recognise the benefits to them that a fully open and inclusive work force delivers. The LGBT community is seeking nothing more than our right to be treated as equal members of the society we help to build.

Mark Peaker, The Peak

16/07/2018

Lam is ignoring public opinion on gay marriage

I am gobsmacked by Chief Executive Carrie Lam Cheng Yuet-ngor's statement as reported by you, that "same-sex marriage was an issue that lacked societal consensus" ("'Same-sex court ruling does not mean we will approve gay marriage in near future,' Hong Kong's leader says", July 12).

For a chief executive to make such a divisive comment beggars belief. Perhaps Lam should spend some time looking at what has happened around the world and the acceptance of same-sex marriage in societies where inclusion of diversity is seen as a fundamental human right.

Lam clearly has no desire to listen to the groundswell of Hong Kong public opinion that has moved decidedly towards the acceptance of same-sex marriage as well as recognising the LGBT community's right to equality. Lam needs to start speaking in a manner that is inclusive of all Hong Kong citizens rather than sideline an issue based on her personal views.

Mark Peaker, The Peak

Why closeting LGBT books is no small matter

This is in response to G. Bailey's misguided interpretation of the issues facing the LGBT community ("Why LGBT outrage over library books is absurd", July 20).

Your correspondent implies that, because there is no "gay bashing" in Hong Kong, the community should remain silent.

The voice of any disadvantaged minority group in Hong Kong echoes loudly, because we are disproportionately marginalised by the community at large in seeking equality. The issue of gay bashing may not be prevalent, but Mr Bailey is wholly wrong to imply that it exists "in their imagination, perhaps", but nowhere else here.

As education is the foundation of understanding, by denying access to LGBT literature ("LGBT-themed books removed from library shelves", June 20) we fail those who need to understand themselves, as well as others whose jaundiced opinion may be based on ignorance.

Mark Peaker, The Peak

Chance for HK to show it is an inclusive city

In taking their case to the Court of Final Appeal, Angus Leung Chun-kwong and his partner Scott Adams give Hong Kong a chance to show it is an inclusive city where stereotypical prejudices are not tolerated ("Gay civil servant will take case to Hong Kong's top court in final bid to win spousal benefits for husband", July 26).

Cuba recently took steps to legalise same-sex marriage by redefining its constitution to amend outmoded wording, from marriage being defined as "the voluntary established union between a man and a woman" to "a consensual union between two people". Gender will thus be eliminated from the definition.

What prevents Hong Kong from doing the same? Homero Acosta, Secretary of the Cuban Council of State, said that the lawmakers studied international laws to have a better understanding of human rights and to prevent any form of discrimination.

According to media reports, Acosta said: "The state has to educate our people on the principles of equality, and support for the most disadvantaged, the elderly, and people with disabilities. It is a principle of [the] social justice and humanism of our system."

Hong Kong's Court of Final Appeal must set aside personal convictions and uphold the same standards as the rest of the international community. Failure to do so will set a precedent for Hong Kong continuing to be a city where discrimination prevails.

Mark Peaker, The Peak

Is FCC creating news instead of reporting it?

The furore surrounding the Foreign Correspondents Club's (FCC) invitation to Andy Chan Ho-tin, founder of the Hong Kong National Party, is justified ("CY Leung dares FCC to surrender lease in row over Andy Chan talk", August 6).

Freedom of speech is a privilege that comes with responsibilities. And while former chief executive Leung Chun-ying has demonstrated enormous ineptness in his veiled threat to link the rent of the club's premises to freedom of speech, he is right to question the validity of this speaker's intentions.

Censorship is not the enemy of freedom of speech.

British subjects have a negative right to freedom of expression, inferring a right to say what they wish within certain parameters – should I elect to stand at Speakers' Corner in Hyde Park and advocate the abolition of the monarchy, for instance, I could be arrested!

It is entirely right for Chief Executive Carrie Lam Yuet-ngor to describe the club's invitation as "regrettable and inappropriate", and for her to reiterate the position of the government in defending Hong Kong as an inalienable part of China.

The FCC (of which I am a member) has sought to inflame sentiment by inviting an individual seeking to damage Hong Kong by advocating independence.

It seems puerile and makes me wonder if the club is trying to create news rather than report it.

Mark Peaker, The Peak

Street cleaners quick to rally morning after

The morning after a super typhoon, our amazing street cleaners are in place sweeping up tonnes of debris.

Overnight, the sound of chainsaws could be heard, as the fire service immediately started clearing away fallen trees.

By tomorrow, it will be like nothing happened!

There has been too much focus on the division of Hong Kong. It takes a super typhoon to show us how united we stand.

Mark Peaker, The Peak

Mallet decision neither "chilling" nor "troubling"

The Hong Kong Immigration Department's decision not to renew the visa of the *Financial Times'* Asia news editor, Victor Mallet, is neither "chilling" nor "deeply troubling". Mr Mallet chose to host an event that confronted the sovereignty of China not in his capacity as a journalist, but as first vice-president of the Foreign Correspondents' Club; he was not reporting news, he was creating it.

Mr Mallet chose to ignore government requests to cancel a talk by Andy Chan Ho-tin, leader of the now-banned Hong Kong National Party, and instead provided a platform for an extremist. The talk also ignited division in Hong Kong, including protests by people who objected to the FCC's hosting of the event. Judging by comments from readers and others in your newspaper, many do not support Mr Mallet.

Freedom of speech is not an invitation to challenge the sovereignty of a nation. The West seems intent on painting

Hong Kong as a city suffering under Chinese interference, but the truth is rather different.

A poll of people in the streets of Hong Kong would find many condemning Mr Mallet, Mr Chan and others who seek to undermine our city's place within China.

Mark Peaker, The Peak

Cathay is also a victim in case of data breach

The cyberattack on Cathay Pacific is a reality of the times in which we live. The sophistication and organisation of hackers means they continue to find ways to hack corporate or government systems with increasing regularity and ease ("Cathay Pacific cyberattack far worse than thought, carrier admits", November 12).

The United Kingdom recently completed implementation of the General Data Protection Regulation, to comply with the standardisation of data protection laws across all 28 European Union countries, which imposes strict new rules on controlling and processing personally identifiable information.

It is time for Asia to adopt similar standards.

Cathay Pacific is a victim of an attack carried out by stealth on a business that has invested heavily in data protection. The airline will continue to invest, but outmanoeuvring those intent on causing harm will never be foolproof.

Mark Peaker, The Peak

Look beyond the labels and gay prejudice

Stuart Heaver writes kindly of the stigma facing LGBT youth who are coming to terms with their sexuality ("Ignorance, Chinese values, religious dogma: LGBT Hong Kong students' plight", November 29).

In a world that has become increasingly tolerant of diversity, there are still ingrained prejudices. Homosexuality is more than sex! It is wholly inaccurate to assume gay men sleep around more than straight men, although that is an accusation often made.

Nor does one's sexuality define one's identity: I am gay; I ski, play golf and squash; I abhor the colour pink. I have straight friends who tremble at the thought of skiing, love disco and adore pink!

If being a butch lesbian is stereotypical, then perhaps my mother was a lesbian, for she certainly had a love of leather jackets and denim trousers. Of course, the most damning accusation levelled by the ignorant against the LGBT community is that most child molesters are gay men: not true!

Crime statistics have shown there are more female than male victims of child molestation.

Furthermore, the LGBT community is about more than sexuality. We are teachers, doctors, pilots, taxi drivers; we are your sons and daughters, your brothers and sisters; we are part of the family of humanity. It is time to look beyond sexuality and understand the person.

Mark Peaker, The Peak

2019

Cheng's actions undermine faith in the judiciary

The behaviour of Secretary for Justice Teresa Cheng Yeuk-wah beggars belief ("Justice chief isn't just wrong about CY Leung case, she's arrogant and clueless", December 31). As does the endorsement by Chief Executive Carrie Lam Cheng Yuet-ngor of her condescending disregard for legitimate questions, reflecting a surprisingly woeful inability to respect the sentiment of the Hong Kong people ("Carrie Lam backs justice minister's decision in CY Leung case", December 28).

The justice secretary is a civil servant. As such, she serves the people, not herself. The law may not be subjective to emotional interpretation, but politics are.

In Teresa Cheng, we have a person whose inability to comprehend this undermines confidence in the judicial system. Our chief executive, in paragraph 2.14 – titled Judicial Independence – of her election manifesto, told us how the chief justice has "spared no effort to maintain the high quality and standards of our judicial officers", and promised full government support.

It would seem that Carrie Lam's election slogan of "We Connect" has been disengaged.

Mark Peaker, The Peak

Golf course is an open space that benefits all

In the ludicrous pursuit of destroying the open green spaces of the Hong Kong Golf Club, perhaps those keen on its demise might want to remove their own lungs, then see how long they survive ("Digging up Fanling golf course a preferred option to boost housing", December 19).

Let's set aside the prejudice that the golf club is merely a playground for tycoons, and understand that this open space benefits all of Hong Kong and, in particular, the residents of Fanling-Sheung Shui New Town.

Mark Peaker, The Peak

Steady hands at controls return Cathay to profit

Cathay Pacific has survived the turbulence and posted profits in excess of analysts' predictions ("Cathay Pacific announces HK$2.3 billion net profit for 2018 in a huge turnaround", February 20). The naysayers now have little to scream about, as Cathay's management team, led by CEO Rupert Hogg, have demonstrated their skills in returning our beloved carrier to profit. Cathay is part of Swire and, as such, benefits from a culture of business patience and pragmatism that will continue to see Cathay Pacific remain at the forefront of airline travel; an icon that Hong Kong remains proud of.

Mark Peaker, The Peak

04/03/2019

Officials playing games with our city's future

In the destruction of Fanling's beauty, the pending obliteration of our seascape, the continued folly of white elephant infrastructure development, and the government's inability to tackle issues that ordinary Hong Kong citizens demand – no lead in our drinking water, streets not clogged with illegally parked cars, etc. – one wonders if they plan out our city's future with the same skill as someone playing SimCity. Perhaps to them it's just a game.

Mark Peaker, The Peak

25/03/2019

Charities ensure millions receive HIV treatment

The news that the "London patient" has become the second person to remain free of HIV, after coming off antiretroviral drugs following stem cell treatment for his Hodgkin's lymphoma cancer, is marvellous.

As Hong Kong is about to host the amfAR gala fundraising dinner tonight, it is worth remembering that, away from the glitter of the evening, The Foundation for Aids Research has, since its inception in 1985, raised over US$500 million and awarded more than 3,300 grants to research teams around the world.

The courage of the late Dr Mathilde Krim, amfAR's founding chairman, and Dame Elizabeth Taylor, founding international chairman, to fight an illness that, despite being known as the "gay disease", has devastated the lives of millions, regardless of their sexual orientation, is remarkable.

While HIV is no longer a death sentence for those able to afford their antiretroviral drug treatment, it remains so for millions of people unable to access these medicines. Local charities may lack the fanfare of amfAR, but they are equally vital in the link – ensuring that regional sufferers have access to testing and treatment.

In Myanmar, The Angus McDonald Trust, an HIV-focused charity I support, informed me that my "donation covered the entire programme of sending 40 children to school, as well as providing a framework for them to access their [antiretroviral therapy] drugs, managing their holistic care (counselling, nutritional support) and supplying home-based visits."

HIV isn't a gay disease; of those 40 children, one is eight years old! With the help of us all, and with amfAR continuing its commitment to a "Countdown to a Cure for Aids", we will end this blight on humanity once and for all.

Mark Peaker, The Peak

24/05/2019

Cathay should be applauded for ad campaign

Cathay Pacific should be commended for an advertising campaign that represents the values of humanity – principles that Hong Kong must learn to accept if it is truly to become a world-class city ("Model in Cathay Pacific's banned same-sex advert proud of his role and says big firms may have misjudged Hong Kong public's attitude to sexual orientation", May 20).

The LGBT community, of which I am part, is not about to break out into overt displays of affection, yet it behoves a company of Cathay's stature to remind others that inclusion is the foundation of tolerance, and that is the foundation of decency.

Mark Peaker, The Peak

31/05/2019

Cathay Pacific ad embraces diversity of life

Pro-establishment lawmaker Priscilla Leung Mei-fun is absolutely correct that controversial advertising can "affect the growth of children" and create a "chilling effect".

Without advertising that embraces the diversity of life, accepts our differences and allows freedom of expression and tolerance, children risk growing up to become narrow-minded bigots advocating prejudice and ignorance, do they not?

Mark Peaker, The Peak

Will victory for Angus Leung be a win for HK?

Congratulations to Angus Leung Chun-kwong and Scott Adams on winning their case for equality ("Gay civil servant wins final appeal on spousal benefits for husband in landmark victory for Hong Kong's LGBT community", June 6).

Hong Kong is finally emerging from the shadows of ignorance. I look forward to Chief Executive Carrie Lam Cheng Yuet-ngor praising the court's decision and her recognition we are all equally part of Asia's world city. The Basic Law delivers to Hong Kong "one country, two systems". Same-sex marriage delivers one love, two systems; both require tolerance and understanding.

Mark Peaker, The Peak

Is a protester like an illegally parked car?

There is seemingly a commonality between an illegally parked car and a rioter: the police ignore them both!

Carrie Lam's cowardly retreat into hiding along with our police force's unfathomable retreat from Legco represent neither having the capability to deal with hooliganism run rampant. Hong Kong is better than the cowards who shield their faces and hurl bricks, destroy property and deface the symbolic identity of our city; they do not represent Hong Kong!

Yet, when our chief executive and police commissioner allow these thugs to seize the day, one wonders how they can be judged as competent in their roles to govern our political and lawful future.

Mark Peaker, The Peak

This is not Hong Kong; we are better than this!

No one respects the thugs who stormed the Legislative Council, vandalising property and defacing the bauhinia emblem of our city. They must be brought to justice.

Yet, those who marched in peaceful condemnation of the government, which is increasingly out of touch with the common man, deserve our respect. We need to find a way to heal the festering wound that Chief Executive Carrie Lam Cheng Yuet-ngor opened with her arrogant dismissal of the voices of the judiciary and Hong Kong's citizens.

Prosecuting those who deliberately sought to destroy our city is warranted. Yet, if the greater benefit to healing division can be achieved through amnesty, then let it be so. Let the wounds heal, allowing all Hongkongers to be governed by a government that cares more about them than it does about itself.

Seldom in my life have I witnessed such blatant incompetence from an administration whose job, regardless of any specific bill, is to ensure social and economic harmony.

The entire Executive Council, and Lam in particular, need to take a long, reflective look at themselves and be reminded that the council is there to serve Hong Kong, not rule over it.

Mark Peaker, The Peak

Cathay correct to take stand over disruption

Cathay Pacific has responded magnificently to the disruption caused to 55,000 passengers as a result of the airport closure.

The company is also justified in dismissing the pilots who abused their privilege and contributed to the unrest that threatens the stability of Hong Kong.

Actions have consequences, and I am proud that Cathay Pacific took a stand against intolerable behaviour.

Mark Peaker, The Peak

Carrie Lam will be remembered as worst leader

Chief Executive Carrie Lam has torn the soul of Hong Kong apart, yet she and her Executive Council remain in place. The arrogance of this beggars belief.

She should by now have reshuffled her team and found fresh faces to deal with this disaster. It is unacceptable that no accountability has been levelled at the Executive Council, whose members continue to behave like they share no responsibility for the hatred that is dividing the city.

Lam will be remembered as the worst political leader to have ever assumed office. Pushing Hong Kong into the abyss, as she termed it, is her defining moment.

Mark Peaker, The Peak

01/10/2019

Congress looks for role to play with HK move

The passage of the Hong Kong Human Rights and Democracy Act of 2019 through the Senate and House of Representatives committees is laughable.

The US can be most useful by sounding a consistent line, publicly and privately, on the importance of Hong Kong's autonomy and the preservation of its legal system, civil rights, etc.

Amazingly, it has failed even at that under Donald Trump's presidency. Creating a recurring drama over Hong Kong's status merely sets up an annual exercise in undermining confidence in Hong Kong that will not impress Beijing.

The existing law already makes clear the basis for Hong Kong's status, and therefore provides for revocation if Washington isn't satisfied.

The creation of this act is all about Congress searching for a role to play, but having no understanding of the rules of the game.

Mark Peaker, The Peak

Vote expresses faith in future of Hong Kong

The passion displayed by voters who turned out in massive numbers on Sunday was a shared belief in the future of Hong Kong; not a validation of the anarchy that those who oppose Beijing may think it was.

Chief Executive Carrie Lam must resign, as should several members of her Executive Council. Secretary for Justice Teresa Cheng Yeuk-wah should be the first head to roll; her contempt for the law and her ability to be absent for major legal decisions is completely unacceptable. "Carry on, Carrie" is not an option.

Mark Peaker, The Peak

Forget dialogue, voters spoke at district elections

That violence returned to our streets on Sunday night is hardly surprising, given our chief executive's continued ineptitude.

Does Carrie Lam not realise that while there are some extremists exploiting the situation, there is also genuine and widespread resentment of her, her Executive Council and her refusal to stand up for Hong Kong and for a better life for Hongkongers?

We need a leader who can bridge social divisions in our city and heal a hatred borne in part by ignorance and fuelled by a lack of belief in a future that this administration is incapable of assuring us will be filled with opportunity.

Lam's declaration that Beijing doesn't hold her accountable only reflects her utter contempt for Hong Kong. How she can blindly refuse to accept accountability for her mistakes beggars belief.

She speaks of dialogue, yet does not realise that people have spoken through the ballot boxes.

On March 14, 2017, during a televised debate with then chief executive contender John Tsang Chun-wah, Lam made the following declaration:

"I trust Hongkongers 100 per cent. If the mainstream opinion is different to mine, I could accept the majority's opinion. If mainstream opinion makes me no longer able to continue the job as chief executive, I'll resign."

Why then, Carrie Lam, are you still chief executive, when the criteria for your removal, as described by yourself, has been met?

Mark Peaker, The Peak

2020

The truth about LGBT support is there to see

Your correspondent Michelle Ma's veiled homophobia reflects only her ignorance ("Research fails to reveal rise in LGBT support", January 16).

If she wants to see how acceptance of LGBTQi has drastically improved in Hong Kong, she should ask the question at the next mass rally.

I would expect a significant majority of the youth gathered would resoundingly prove her wrong.

Mark Peaker, The Peak

Carrie Lam is keeping herself busy in Davos

Since Hong Kong's fall "into an abyss", which our own chief executive feigned tears over, she has found time to attend the enthronement of the Japanese emperor and is presently wrapped up in furs attending the Davos summit – our very own junket queen indeed!

Meanwhile, Ocean Park stands to get HK$10 billion to reward incompetence!

To borrow from a Disney character, that is simply "Goofy".

Mark Peaker, The Peak

No excuse for xenophobia against Chinese

The unprecedented hysteria over the novel coronavirus pneumonia outbreak highlights mostly the prejudicial ignorance of those seeking to condemn Chinese individuals as carriers of some deadly plague.

The sickening sight of xenophobia barring innocent Chinese nationals from restaurants, toilet facilities and subway seats, and causing people to be spat on in the streets, reflects a society that has lost its moral compass.

Ignorance is no excuse for hatred and, when this virus has faded away, the nations of the world owe the people of China two words: "We're sorry".

Mark Peaker, The Peak

LGBT housing debate reveals an urban myth

I refer to Abraham Chan Lok-shung SC's appalling comment that the government was entitled to deny public housing to same-sex couples because there were not enough flats to meet the demand of the city's low-income residents ("Hong Kong's public housing ban on gay couples unconstitutional, court rules", March 4). His comments expose the misconception that members of the LGBT community are all middle class, wrapped in the privilege of the pink dollar and immune to the needs of other low-income citizens.

I have been critical of company diversity and inclusion programmes that often reflect well-educated, middle-class members of our community, but do not reach out to those who have no one to discuss their sexual orientation or gender identification with.

I am less interested in an investment banker using their sexual orientation as a path to career progression than those trapped within an environment where no one hears them scream.

LGBT issues reach into every family in Hong Kong, often hidden from view and leading to depression, suicide and the destruction of lives. Our government should be seeking to heal division across the breadth of those who make up our city, not seeking to treat one sector as second class.

Being LGBT is not defined by wealth, and we need to ensure this ruling gives hope to those in our community who – through access to affordable housing – can begin to build the first steps of their own identity, secure in the fact they are accepted for who they are.

Mark Peaker, The Peak

Silence speaks volumes for Western media

It is interesting to note Kurt Tong's, the former US consul general to Hong Kong, comment on the city government's good handling of the coronavirus situation yet receiving "zero credit" for it ("Fallout from pandemic clouds Hong Kong's economic future, Kurt Tong says", March 17).

It is also worth noting that Western media, who during the protests reported night and day on the masked rioters, have said little about Hong Kong's excellent handling of the pandemic. Foreign bias unmasked, perhaps?

Mark Peaker, The Peak

Bars' last orders should have been weeks ago

Chief Executive Carrie Lam Cheng Yuet-ngor's inability to get ahead of the Covid-19 spread in Hong Kong is demonstrated by her clumsy self-proclaimed decision to initially ban the sale of all alcohol (dropped amid a backlash), only to be followed by the delayed closure of all pubs and bars.

If hindsight were an Olympic sport, Lam would win gold!

As Allan Zeman, chairman of Lan Kwai Fong Group, comments: "Business has been bad in the district for the last few weeks, so whether it's open or closed, it does not make a big difference."

Had Lam acted proactively, she could have closed pubs and clubs a few weeks ago and stemmed the local spread of the virus. Maybe then we would be emerging from this nightmare, as opposed to enduring it for longer than necessary.

Mark Peaker, The Peak

18/04/2020

China deserves praise for giving world warning

Dr Chi Wang argues that China's cover-up of the coronavirus crisis has lost the country trust. Really? History shows that no country has ever leapt to announce a new pathogen outbreak.

Initially, China was no different. But rather than blaming China, Dr Wang should hold China up as a beacon of success for stemming the spread domestically and giving the world ample warning to prepare.

On January 4, the head of the Chinese Centre for Disease Control and Prevention talked by phone with the director of the US Centers for Disease Control and Prevention about the pneumonia outbreak. The two sides agreed to keep in close contact for information-sharing cooperation.

It is implausible that the United States was unaware of events, relying solely on the WHO [World Health Organization] for access to privileged information. Donald Trump continued to play down the threat posed to America, ignored the signs and put his own citizens at risk!

The US president remained dismissive. On February 26, ignoring the facts, he declared, "When you have 15 people, and the 15 within a couple of days is going to be down too close to zero, that's a pretty good job we've done," before prophesying on the 27th that, "one day, it's like a miracle, it will disappear".

China made grievous mistakes, yet took steps to ensure that these do not reoccur.

Dr Li Wenliang's death and the circumstances that prevented him from speaking openly about the virus have pricked China's conscience.

President Trump refuses to allow Dr Anthony Fauci, head of the National Institute of Allergy and Infectious Diseases, to answer questions when he does not like Fauci's answers.

So, who is suppressing whom?

Mark Peaker, The Peak

18/06/2020

Flagship carrier deserves to be preserved

The naysayers are bemoaning the government's massive bailout of Cathay Pacific, condemning the use of their money to rescue a private enterprise.

This is hogwash. Cathay Pacific has acted as our city's flagship carrier for decades, bereft of the benefits other carriers enjoyed as it offered world-class service and safety records.

When other airlines went belly-up, it was Cathay Pacific that came to the rescue of stranded Hongkongers and brought them home.

Cathay Pacific is part of the pulse of our city, employing more than 33,000 people, supporting charities and easily the most recognisable emblem of Hong Kong overseas.

In this time of extreme turbulence, it is right that the government supports the survival of a company that exemplifies the best of Hong Kong.

Mark Peaker, The Peak

06/07/2020

US' preaching on national security falls flat

US Consul General Hanscom Smith describes the new national security legislation as a "terrible" law but offers scant reasoning for his statement ("'Terrible' law will not change how US consulate operates, top US envoy says", July 3). Foreign governments decry our remarkably restrained police action as brutality but stay silent when their own forces unleash harsher punishment themselves.

The US has 17 agencies that collaborate to gather intelligence for national security and foreign relations activities, including the CIA, the FBI, the Department of Homeland Security, the Department of State and the Department of the Treasury.

Would the consul general describe all of these agencies, their laws and their international reach as "terrible", or is it only acceptable for his country to enact laws that protect national security?

Mark Peaker, The Peak

19/07/2020

Australia less alluring than one may think

Scott Morrison, Australia's prime minister, seeks to entice young Hongkongers fleeing the imagined tyranny of Beijing's national security legislation by offering them a pathway to permanent residency ("Australia offers Hongkongers pathway to permanent residency", July 9).

It will be interesting to see how many take up his offer; the allure of high taxes, a population intolerant of Asians and an economy entering a downturn is not as appealing as he may think.

Hong Kong remains at the heart of the Pearl River Delta's growth, and the low taxation and career opportunities, combined with a lifestyle far more diverse than the sunburned country offers, may mean saying "G'day" will never be as attractive as "ni hao ma".

Mark Peaker, The Peak

25/07/2020

Non-isolation of crews requires an explanation

Can Carrie Lam explain why, under her guidance, for she is the chief executive, she allowed aircrew flying in from high-infection areas and seamen aboard vessels already known to be cesspits of contagion to freely enter our city without the mandatory 14-day quarantine everyone else was subjected to?

Mark Peaker, The Peak

15/09/2020

Scottish leader gets it right on British PM

Bravo to Nicola Sturgeon for expressing her contempt (shared by us all) for the British prime minister. Boris Johnson's intent to break international law is abhorrent and reeks of irony ("Brexit is imploding and looks like Boris Johnson is engineering it", September 10).

Johnson's government condemns China for failing to honour its pledge to uphold the rule of law in Hong Kong, yet finds it perfectly OK to undermine the foundation of the Good Friday Agreement to serve his own political ambition.

Mark Peaker, The Peak

Call for equality over same-sex relationships

The battle for LGBT equality in Hong Kong continues. That a claimed "Asia's World City" takes a view on same-sex relationships more akin to Dickensian times would be laughable if it did not destroy the hopes and aspirations of those who seek simply to live their lives free from prejudice.

Mark Peaker, The Peak

Work efficiency reminder of the city we know

We forget, amid all the hatred, just how good our government departments can be and, more importantly, the level of professionalism of those working within. I made a 9.30am booking to replace my Hong Kong identity card with the new smart ID card. By 9.36am, I had been processed. The staff were courteous and utterly professional, even remembering to wish me a good day as I exited.

It is easy to knock our government for its failures at the top, but let's remember to praise those who do their job with dedication and pride – this is the Hong Kong we know and cherish.

Mark Peaker, The Peak

Cathay decision is hard, but will help it survive

As "heart-wrenching" as the decision was to retire the Cathay Dragon brand and let go of 8,500 staff from across the Cathay Pacific group, it was the right decision.

Cathay Pacific has stood with Hong Kong for decades, sewing a thread of community support as well as acting as a safety net for stranded passengers when other airlines failed.

In these most difficult times, it is Hong Kong's moment to understand that the steps the airline is taking now are meant to preserve as many jobs as possible and allow this proud part of our city's heritage to survive.

In survival remains the opportunity for future employment, when the world returns to normalcy and the wings of Cathay shall again carry the pride of Hong Kong around the globe.

Mark Peaker, The Peak

Job cuts were best way to help Cathay survive

Rishi Teckchandani displays a false sense of economy in his analysis of the Cathay Pacific Airways decision to lay off thousands of workers ("Cathay should have been left to market forces", November 12).

Would he have preferred the airline to have failed completely, taking with it all 33,000 jobs, to the restructuring that preserved employment for the majority while offering those who were let go the possibility of re-employment?

Similarly, the government made a strategic investment in Cathay Pacific to ensure that Hong Kong remains a viable transport hub, a decision that was, again, based on the preservation of jobs – and not the bailout that Mr Teckchandani suggests.

The decision to let go of 8,500 staff was the best way to navigate the airline back to profitability, preserving as many jobs as possible.

Mark Peaker, The Peak

28/11/2020

Are *tai tai* wives different from karaoke users?

The largest outbreak of Covid-19 infections is traced to dance clubs, yet the Hong Kong government allows them to remain open. Why? Are the *tai tai* wives different from the common karaoke or bar user?

Mark Peaker, The Peak

09/12/2020

City should not have to rely on luck for vaccine

It is quite bewildering that Professor David Hui Shu-cheong bases his scientific reasoning on luck as he declares, "If we are lucky, by the third quarter of next year we will start seeing the first batches of vaccines arrive, and I believe by around 2022, the chance for all Hongkongers to be vaccinated should be quite high".

This is a wholly unacceptable forecast for Hongkongers and for the economic rebound we need to restore livelihoods and hope. As Britain begins Covid-19 vaccination, perhaps our chief executive might want to stop talking about her "piles of cash at home" and start dealing with acquiring immediate access to vaccinate those at high risk in the city and to allow it to start functioning again.

Lam may feel she has done no wrong. However, if there is one issue that unites our polarised society, it is a shared disdain of a leader Hong Kong finds guilty of taking our home into the abyss. That she also feels it appropriate to tell an interviewer she has "piles of cash at home" when Hongkongers are losing their jobs and unable to pay bills or buy groceries reflects the insensitivity of someone out of touch with reality.

The government's objective for zero local Covid-19 cases is as unachievable as its ridiculous claim to ensure Hong Kong remains one of the world's safest cities for road travel by boasting, "Zero accidents on the road, Hong Kong's goal", but allows illegal parking and the running of red lights to continue unabated.

We need a government with a plan, not merely one that creates meaningless catchphrases.

Mark Peaker, The Peak

192

What about the rights of protest victims in city?

Lord Shinkwin, one assumes, enjoys the ermine and red leather couches of the House of Lords from where he pontificates: "We will not belittle your suffering. We will not forget you."

Perhaps his lordship would like to opine why, during the 150-plus years when Hong Kong was a British colony, it was never a democracy ("Why Britain will continue to speak up for Hong Kong", December 12).

Shinkwin and his band of principled crusaders deify Grandma Wong as a "person of courage and principle", yet say nothing of an elderly man killed by "peaceful protesters" while taking a video of a clash between protesters and local residents, or a passer-by assaulted simply because he wanted to clear the road, and another set on fire because he dared to speak in opposition to the thugs destroying his freedom.

Could his lordship request his All-Party Parliamentary Group on Hong Kong to ask that those responsible be brought to justice?

Shinkwin declares Hong Kong is suffering from draconian laws, and China is in breach of the Joint Declaration, yet conveniently ignores Britain's own Official Secrets Act.

As a long-term resident of Hong Kong, I remain confident of our city's future as a key and dynamic city within China. The rest of the world may wish to continue playing politics with Hong Kong, but Hong Kong has more important business – as part of the world's most vibrant economic growth area – to be getting on with.

Mark Peaker, The Peak

2021

Failures of Lam are reason for "powder keg"

With reference to "Hong Kong youth anger could again explode into social unrest, experts warn" (January 5) and a survey by two universities finding simmering grievances are a "powder keg waiting to go off", Hong Kong's real frustrations are not over our relationship with Beijing but with our relationship with Carrie Lam.

The Chief Executive has shown scant regard for the woes of the people she represents. Her account of having "piles of cash" in her upstairs drawer (since she is denied banking services due to US sanctions) is at odds with those who have lost their jobs and are facing financial ruin.

For her to state that she welcomes the national security law because it allows the government to focus on getting back to business reflects her inability to govern ("Unapologetic over last year's protests, Hong Kong leader 'back to her old self' and ready to take on pandemic", November 29). Regardless of the unacceptable violence and destruction during the protests, her role was to ensure the government continued to function.

Hong Kong is a city filled with talent, yet we have a government that refuses to see it. Our chief executive fails as a leader because she has no ability to listen and even less to communicate.

Hong Kong deserves more.

Mark Peaker, The Peak

Will Carrie Lam lead the way on Chinese vaccine?

Can we assume Chief Executive Carrie Lam Cheng Yuet-ngor will take the first jab of the Sinovac vaccine publicly to prove its safety to the people of Hong Kong?

Mark Peaker, The Peak

Hiccups merely symptom of a deeper malaise

Carrie Lam Cheng Yuet-ngor's comment that Hong Kong is experiencing "hiccups" in the procurement of the three vaccines already purchased by the city serves as a sweeping condemnation of her inability to have the correct vaccines procured and at the correct time!

The world's biggest vaccination campaign has begun, with more than 82.5 million doses in 59 countries having been administered, an average of 3.95 million doses a day. Why then has Hong Kong, a rich, compact First World city, neither administered a single shot nor drawn up a timeline for vaccination?

This is a damning reflection upon a chief executive and her ministerial appointments. Hong Kong could have been the first city in the world to be fully vaccinated; we could have, for once, been Asia's World City!

Instead, we are lagging behind Third World economies.

Mark Peaker, The Peak

City lost none of the freedoms that matter

Your correspondent Tom Yam opines, "those in the ruling class like Mr Chan do not seem to understand the impact that the national security law and the ensuing actions of the SAR government have had on many Hong Kong people" ("Hongkongers choosing the UK seek more than a good living", February 17).

An example of what Hongkongers have lost since the introduction of the national security law would be appropriate. However, it is difficult to find, as the reality is that little has changed.

You can still criticise the government, you can still call our chief executive ineffective, you can still protest peacefully if permission has police approval – something also required under colonial rule. Yes, you can no longer terrorise innocent citizens, kill them with bricks, set them aflame and destroy property simply because you feel your view is the only legitimate one.

Hong Kong is a city within China, we must strive to ensure it is the best city, taking full advantage of the economic opportunity our position in the Pearl River Delta offers.

Hong Kong retains all its privileges, bar for those who seek to destroy it with demands for independence and foreign interference. It is naive to claim that our freedoms are being eroded. The grass may seem greener on the other side: it never is.

Mark Peaker, The Peak

Homosexuality ruling reveals deep ignorance

The utter obliviousness of a Chinese provincial court in upholding a ruling describing homosexuality as "a psychological disorder" reflects more its own ignorance. Perhaps they need to study their own history to understand that homosexuality and same-sex relationships in China date from the Shang dynasty, 16th to 11th century BCE.

The term *luan feng* was used to describe homosexuality, which was largely viewed with indifference and treated with openness. Ironically, it was the westernisation of China that saw opposition to homosexuality increase during the 19th and 20th centuries.

It is also a fact that in 1997 all mentions of homosexuality in criminal law were removed, and in 2001 the Chinese Society of Psychiatry declassified homosexuality as a mental disorder. However, as is also common in the West, acceptance of diversity often fails to filter down to provincial areas.

Hong Kong is not immune from this: our government's own inadequacy in dealing with LGBTQi issues was highlighted in July 2018 when Carrie Lam stated same-sex marriage was an issue that lacked societal consensus, despite overwhelming support for it in Hong Kong.

As a gay man, I have witnessed the tremendous strides our community has made in being accepted not for whom we sleep with, but merely for who we are and the valuable contributions we make to society around the world.

Joe Jackson sang, " ... don't call me a faggot, not unless you are a friend". I am heartened that in China and around the world, we have more friends than those who, through their own narrow-mindedness, seek to destroy.

Mark Peaker, The Peak

British envoy brings clarity, not confusion

Former Hong Kong British consul general Caroline Wilson has seemingly fallen foul of Beijing's control over what can and cannot be said ("China summons British ambassador over her 'inappropriate' article", March 10).

It is an unfortunate situation as Dame Caroline is a person who sees the best in all, regardless of political policy or party loyalty.

In opining that those who report about China do not hate China, she brings clarity to the confusion that not every criticism is a condemnation.

For China to accept criticism shows a maturity that has seemingly been lost in the past few years.

It is, however, perhaps understandable when no one believes the answers proffered, even when they are truthful. Chinese media censors but seldom makes false claims or sensationalises Western topics, but the same cannot be said of Western media and the spread of fake news, such as the blatant misreporting on Hong Kong.

Clarity of communication is vital; appreciating that when China answers it is honest is precisely that maturity of dialogue the West must understand and precisely why having Dame Caroline as ambassador bodes well for China-UK trade as well as culture, economic diplomacy and development.

Mark Peaker, The Peak

Authorities deserve thanks for their effort

Having received my first jab of BioNTech at St Paul's Hospital, one can attest personally to the brilliant quality of care and professionalism administered.

From arrival to injection and departure, the process was effortless, from the smiling lift operator to the nurses, the service was world-class.

In fact, for once one felt proud that Hong Kong really is Asia's World City.

Bravo to the Department of Health.

Mark Peaker, The Peak

Time to stop interfering and let HK be HK

For US Consul General Hanscom Smith to suggest the solution for Hong Kong is letting the city "be itself" ("Letting Hong Kong be itself offers best hope for city's future", April 2), he might want to call United States senators Marco Rubio, Tom Cotton and Ted Cruz or former Secretary of State Mike Pompeo and ask them to refrain from interfering in every aspect of the city to allow Hong Kong to "be itself".

Hong Kong is part of China, a proud city that will stand tall as the key player within the Pearl River Delta.

We neither seek nor need advice from a country that takes the moral high ground on the backs of broken communities within its own borders.

Mark Peaker, The Peak

Poor American policing back in the spotlight

United States President Joe Biden opines: "There is absolutely no justification, none, for looting. Peaceful protests – understandable", in response to the fatal shooting of a black man by a police officer ("Daunte Wright death: Minnesota officer who pulled trigger meant to draw taser, police chief says", April 13).

Perhaps he should be declaring, "There is absolutely no justification for the murder of innocent citizens, none. Peaceful policing – obligatory."

Mark Peaker, The Peak

Spare British arrivals from 21-day isolation

I heeded the government's request to get vaccinated and have received both shots of the BioNTech vaccine. Like many, I considered this my civic duty to help the city recover and get business flowing again. However, what is the point when our government continues to play hindsight policy with its out-of-touch reaction to the ever-changing global improvements in the Covid-19 vaccination rate?

I am no better off being vaccinated than not in terms of how Chief Executive Carrie Lam Cheng Yuet-ngor's ministers treat individuals. I could fly to Britain, a country that has astounded the world with its successful vaccination roll-out, so successful that it no longer ranks Covid-19 as the leading cause of death (it dropped to the third-highest cause in March) and experts have said Britain is no longer in a pandemic situation but at "endemic" levels.

However, the Hong Kong government has failed to react at all, insisting returnees from Britain endure the 21-day quarantine requirement, which must be served at the government-dictated hotel, the Rambler Garden Hotel in Tsing Yi. Some guests have raised complaints about the size of the rooms and their cleanliness.

If the government had any concern for the restoration of business, it needs to move swiftly in reaction to both the negative impact of the pandemic as well as the positive. Why should people get vaccinated when the government fails to offer any benefit?

Mark Peaker, The Peak

18/05/2021

Australia biting hand that's fed economic boom

The Australian government's reaction to China's decision to indefinitely suspend high-level economic dialogue with Australia reflects Canberra's naivety in biting the hand of the country that has played a significant part in Australia's economic boom.

The development is seemingly a reaction to Australia's federal government revoking the state of Victoria's participation in China's Belt and Road Initiative. One wonders why Australia is feeling aggrieved? It is time for Australia to understand there is more to foreign diplomacy than "G'day".

Mark Peaker, The Peak

Time to make vaccination mandatory

It is the law that we pay taxes, have a driving licence, require a passport for travel, carry and produce our identity card when required, and obey all the laws that make Hong Kong a safe, civilised city.

The government had no qualms about mandating that domestic helpers get vaccinated in order to have their contracts renewed. While this reeked of racism and snobbery, and was eventually withdrawn, it proved the government can act.

It is disgusting that up to 2 million vaccine doses run the risk of expiring and will be discarded. This is a shameful condemnation of both Secretary for Food and Health Professor Sophia Chan Siu-chee and Chief Executive Carrie Lam Cheng Yuet-ngor and their continued inability to connect with Hong Kong.

Their failure reveals the fact that vaccination must be made mandatory for every Hong Kong resident. Failing to get vaccinated is not a political stance, it is a failing of people against their friends, families and Hong Kong.

Many of us accept our glorious city is a part of China. However, Beijing's insistence that patriots govern is only half the answer.

The city suffers not from its ties with the mainland but rather from the failings of a chief executive who, as youth lose employment, thinks it fine to comment she has too much cash at home, and a secretary for food and health who oversaw the procurement of food that made some returnees staying at a quarantine centre unwell.

Beijing may demand patriots, we demand competence.

Mark Peaker, The Peak

Legislator's slur on Gay Games is uncalled for

In commenting that he does "respect people with different sexual orientation. Whatever you do in your room, it's your own business. But if you do it in public, it's disgraceful", Hong Kong lawmaker Junius Ho Kwan-yiu appears to believe the Gay Games is a massive orgy ("Regina Ip backs Hong Kong Gay Games, but others say it's 'disgraceful'", June 10).

Being gay doesn't mean being promiscuous, there is more to us than sex.

Hong Kong's successful Gay Games hosting bid, and it will be the first Asian city to do so, has failed to make headway with the Home Affairs Bureau and Leisure and Cultural Services Department in securing venues: that is an error of planning and one they hope can be resolved.

To have a government representative label the event as "dirty money" is wholly unacceptable, and Junius Ho should be forced to apologise.

Hong Kong, as Asia's supposed "world city", needs to embrace diversity and our chief executive should be welcoming any plans to boost the morale and economic opportunities for Hong Kong, regardless of whether it is the pink dollar or pink renminbi.

Mark Peaker, The Peak

Government's efforts have failed workers

Chief Secretary Matthew Cheung Kin-chung is completely misguided, as are Professor Sophia Chan Siu-chee and Chief Executive Carrie Lam Cheng Yuet-ngor, if they believe their pandemic policies place "public health as paramount".

Despite our city's vast wealth, the most vulnerable of our society have suffered disproportionately as a result of government's one-size-fits-all pandemic policy.

Low-paying jobs have disappeared, parents and children have been confined to minuscule homes, and domestic workers and poor elderly placed at heightened risk of exposure.

The government response has been to funnel money into businesses instead of directly to workers, which has worsened the financial security of the city's working class and placed undue mental health strain upon them.

Hong Kong might have one of the lowest incidences of, and deaths per capita from, Covid-19.

That is because the city is shut down and cut off from the lifeline of business that it is founded on. It is neither sustainable nor healthy.

Cheung praises his government for having been "working at full steam since February".

Indeed, it has. The problem is that Hong Kong is a digital city declining under an analogue government.

Mark Peaker, The Peak

01/07/2021

City blind to the success of UK vaccine roll-out

It is hardly a surprise to see the Hong Kong government's overreaction to the Delta variant in the United Kingdom: in banning the entry of all flights from Britain and barring entry for anyone who has spent more than two hours in the country in the preceding 21 days. This knee-jerk reaction places the same restrictions as imposed before any vaccine roll-outs were undertaken.

The reimposition of these draconian measures reflects a health minister and government that have failed to take in the success of the vaccination programme in the United Kingdom. It is clear the Delta variant is surging in the country, yet hospitalisation and deaths remain at a trickle.

As the United Kingdom continues its world-beating vaccination implementation, something Hong Kong has failed to achieve, the country remains on course for the alleviation of all Covid-19 restrictions on July 19.

Hong Kong, however, chooses to continue its hit-and-hope policy, offering zero benefit for persons who are fully vaccinated.

Hong Kong cannot shut itself away forever, and we need an exit plan that accepts the risks of Covid-19 balanced alongside the global vaccination achievement.

Mark Peaker, The Peak

05/07/2021

No excuse for July 1 attack on police officer

There is no validation for the attempted murder of a police officer, that the assailant is dead robs us all of justice.

The silence of the Australian, British and American governments in failing to condemn this senseless act of violence further reflects the duplicity of their views that those who carry out acts of violence in the name of democracy are somehow above the law.

The Hong Kong Police Force continues to proudly protect our home, and officers cannot be allowed to be in fear of their lives in the conduct of their duty.

Mark Peaker, The Peak

What the city demands is competence

It is unacceptable to the people of Hong Kong that our No. 2 official should lack policy experience across a range of issues that affect the daily lives of citizens ("Hong Kong No 2 official John Lee's focus is on national security, not other policy issues, Carrie Lam says", July 11).

While the fact that Chief Executive Carrie Lam Cheng Yuet-ngor is making poverty alleviation and issues concerning ethnic minority groups secondary concerns is unacceptable, that she chooses to also make our city's youth – in other words, our city's future – a secondary issue is unforgivable.

There is more to Hong Kong than the national security law. That is something that is being handled perfectly well by the central government's liaison office.

John Lee Ka-chiu has been appointed to an office which requires oversight of Hong Kong for the benefit of all Hongkongers ("Hong Kong's new No 2 official John Lee dismisses concerns over policy experience", June 26).

For Lam to announce that "we will play to our strengths respectively, with me spending more effort on these aspects" is wholly inappropriate, as they remain areas where she has already failed to make a difference.

Beijing is right to demand patriots, but Hong Kong demands competence.

Mark Peaker, The Peak

Carrie Lam is out of touch on LGBT issues

Chief Executive Carrie Lam Cheng Yuet-ngor might not understand the meaning of a pluralistic society. It is a society where people's values are appreciated, a society where two or more groups coexist with respect and friendship. That she uses the word but then describes the LGBT community as "them" – saying "Hong Kong society does not have a consensus on giving them any legal status or further rights" – reveals her obliviousness to reality.

Her time as chief executive has seen our home divided, as she has failed time and again to listen to the mood of the people. Her tenure has been to the detriment of Hong Kong people whose voices have been ignored by a leader who is incapable of listening.

In a pluralistic society, diversity places a pronounced emphasis on aspects of dialogue with other positions. It incorporates values, it remains open and asks questions about meaning and understanding. It reminds and challenges us about where we go, what we do and why.

Hongkongers have a voice, the LGBT community has a voice, and it is clear people increasingly accept same-sex relationships. The only part that is "very, very controversial" is our chief executive's refusal to accept this.

Mark Peaker, The Peak

Verdict shows limit to freedom of expression

Tong Ying-kit has been found guilty of terrorism and inciting secession. Opposition activist Nathan Law Kwun-chung decries the verdict, saying it shows the authorities are using the judicial system to suppress freedom of expression, opining that "a sense of white terror continues to linger in Hong Kong". He is wrong.

Tong drove his bike into a line of police officers; regardless of the speed, those officers' lives were placed at risk. His revolutionary flag was visible to all and was seen as a symbol designed to provoke further hatred against our city's police force.

Freedom of speech is not absolute. When Eleanor Roosevelt held aloft the Universal Declaration of Human Rights (1948), its wording stated, "Everyone has the right to freedom of opinion and expression; this right includes freedom to hold opinions without interference and to seek, receive and impart information and ideas through any media regardless of frontiers." However, the International Covenant on Civil and Political Rights, which also enshrines the right to freedom of opinion and expression, clarifies this right with the words, "subject to certain restrictions".

Hong Kong's national security law adopts a similar set of restrictions where anyone seeking to incite violence or acts of sedition may be prosecuted.

Hong Kong isn't dying, businesses – unlike Nathan Law – are not fleeing and our city shall emerge from the shadows of those attempting to destabilise it, stronger and prouder in our role as China's greatest city.

Mark Peaker, The Peak

HK must never venture down the Afghan path

As the US flees Afghanistan, allowing the murderous Taliban to rise again, we see the failure of American foreign policy ("China, Russia embassies stay put in Afghanistan as US allies flee Taliban", August 16).

Those who waved US flags on the streets of Hong Kong should be reminded that Washington's foreign policy serves only one aim – its own.

The ideology of a country seeking to impose its flawed values on another shall never succeed. Afghanistan is America's failure and Hong Kong shall not follow the same path.

Mark Peaker, The Peak

Road safety must start with better driving

The deaths of two people caused by a taxi driver who slammed into a pedestrian island on Kwong Fuk Road is tragic ("Hong Kong taxi driver in Tai Po crash that killed 2 charged with dangerous driving causing death", August 24). That a few others remain in hospital is a worrying reminder of the low driving standards of Hong Kong taxis and the government's ludicrous policy of "Zero accidents on the road, Hong Kong's goal".

This government seems to have done nothing to improve the driving standards of those tasked with carrying members of the public nor to ensure people can cross roads legally without fear of being hit by drivers who run red lights.

Taxis remain adorned with illegally mounted banks of mobile phones fixed to their dashboards, and taxi drivers fail to indicate, illegally stop to pick up or drop off, illegally park and illegally idle their engines. They show no care or concern for their passengers or pedestrians.

The Road Safety Council is chaired by the Deputy Commissioner of Police (Operations), and is committed to reducing the number and severity of traffic accidents in Hong Kong by formulating road safety initiatives and undertaking education and publicity programmes to encourage everyone to take up responsibility to ensure the safety of every road user. Yet people are dying as a result of a failure of enforcement and a disregard for public safety in the face of worsening driving standards in Hong Kong.

Mark Peaker, The Peak

Lawmaker out of step with city on Gay Games

It is as pointless as it is exhausting responding to the homophobic hatred that flows from the mouth of Junius Ho Kwan-yiu ("Hong Kong Gay Games 'a wolf in sheep's clothing' and threat to national security, lawmakers warn", August 25). One wonders where his hatred of homosexuals stems from. His attempt to politicise the Gay Games reflects his own ignorance, but he shames Hong Kong, a city where the people are fortunately far more tolerant than him.

Mark Peaker, The Peak

Deal allowing mainland visitors in was poorly negotiated

Chief Executive Carrie Lam Cheng Yuet-ngor has once again displayed her inability to be an effective negotiator. In agreeing to allow 2,000 visitors daily from Guangdong and Macau to enter the city with no quarantine, she has effectively played her only card, with zero benefit to Hongkongers who are required to quarantine for 14 days upon entering those regions.

Hongkongers have worked hard to bring the pandemic under control here. Yet we continue to pay the price – from BBQ sites that remain closed to no relief from wearing masks outdoors, from families separated to economic hardship.

Hongkongers have for almost two years been subjected to some of the world's toughest quarantine restrictions. Our chief executive states that she "cannot speak for the central government"; could she, however, for once, speak for the people of Hong Kong?

Mark Peaker, The Peak

Gay Games delay tells the world Hong Kong is closed for business

The decision to postpone the Gay Games, originally scheduled for November 2022, for a year reflects the impact of Carrie Lam Yuet-ngor's draconian 21-day quarantine imposition.

Whilst this event might be of scant importance to her or her government, the delay reflects an international perception that Hong Kong is closed for business. This government, with no end plan in sight, has allowed an event scheduled over a year away to fall victim to a policy that serves no one other than government ministers who are immune to the pressure from it.

Has our chief executive, who surely would ask of Hongkongers nothing she would not be prepared to do herself, spent a single day in quarantine? The financial loss to the city caused by the Gay Games delay is part of an enormous financial loss Hong Kong will endure as a result of having a government leader who seems to have a deficient understanding of business.

This ignorance allows her to falsely believe Hong Kong's economy is sustainable and can be driven by domestic consumption; it cannot.

Hong Kong needs an exit strategy. We need to know that our government is leading us towards the resumption of international trade and travel.

It is one thing to have BBQ pits closed, it is quite another to have the city closed because of an impractical belief that Covid-19 can be eradicated. Vaccination was meant to be the key to freedom, Hongkongers have heeded this and we want the doors of our city open and the draconian quarantine measures removed.

Mark Peaker, The Peak

Article 23: Hong Kong must not repeat the mistakes of the 2019 extradition bill fiasco

Article 23 is floating back into view across a sea of divided opinions ("Hong Kong officials urged to speed up delivery of Article 23 security law to counter foreign interference", October 3).

Unlike the national security law that was imposed by the National People's Congress Standing Committee, Article 23 legislation will be enacted by our city's own government. It is therefore imperative that the competence of our chief executive and elected officials improves.

The need for public consultation is core to the success of this legislation and the future peace and prosperity of Hong Kong for all.

The failure of the bill to amend the Fugitive Offenders Ordinance was the result of the government's complete failure to take the time to speak and listen to the community. In seeking to ignore public sentiment and force through in an unacceptably short period of time amendments that citizens saw as an invasion of their own security, the government plunged our city into the abyss, for which our chief executive is entirely to blame.

It is now time for mature dialogue, for the government to understand that laws protect citizens' safety, and to protect our rights against abuses by other people, organisations and by the government itself.

Mark Peaker, The Peak

11/10/2021

Hongkongers deserve credit, not Lam

Chief Executive Carrie Lam Yuet-ngor has delivered her latest policy address and laid out her vision for the future of Hong Kong.

She showed empathy towards herself, graciously accepting the privilege she has enjoyed in being our chief executive. Sadly, it is privilege many in Hong Kong do not share.

Her speech was delivered in her usual manner, akin to a headmistress lecturing students. There was no apology to Hong Kong citizens who bore the brunt of her failure to avert the violence that rocked our city, no thank you for citizens who vaccinated themselves in the now futile belief we were working together to open our borders and restore business confidence, and no praise for families who have endured financial and social distress.

That she later declared, "I love doing things non-stop" echoes again her belief that only she has worked tirelessly to keep Hong Kong moving forward.

She is wrong. That accolade goes to the community leaders, NGOs, small businesses, office workers, nurses, street cleaners and every citizen who has remained committed to ensuring Hong Kong survives beyond the most divisive chief executive we have ever had.

Mark Peaker, The Peak

Row our boat, nurture our talent

If Hong Kong were a Marvel comic, we would relish the vision of the Northern Metropolis and Lantau Tomorrow. But this utopian mirage is somewhat at odds with the reality of Hong Kong today.

A future is built upon a foundation of support for citizens to achieve their best, and this is underpinned by a government that inspires individuals to aspire. Chief Executive Carrie Lam Yuet-ngor may feel she is a visionary and that integration of Hong Kong into the Greater Bay Area makes sense, but buildings are not the heartbeat of communities and infrastructure not the pulse of the people.

For our halcyon days to return, Hong Kong needs a pathway of opportunity that allows the natural talent of our city to blossom and to invigorate entrepreneurial creativity often stymied by a government that consistently fails to nurture talent across a spectrum of industries, from arts and culture to technology.

Hong Kong indeed has much to lose, as President Xi Jinping warned in 2017. If we are not to miss the boat, our government needs to start earnestly paddling for the people it represents.

Mark Peaker, The Peak

03/11/2021

Covid-19 strategy is a tragicomedy

Professor Sophia Chan, secretary for food and health, opines that "'zero-Covid' also puts us on a par with our neighbours and provides a basis for resuming cross-boundary travel and reinvigorating our economy". Really?

Can she then define the timeline for the resumption of cross-boundary travel, given the city has met all the previous targets set, and when the miraculous revival of Hong Kong's economy will happen, given that her support of the medically unproven 21-day quarantine has severely hit business in the city?

Shakespeare said of his players, "Speak the speech, I pray you, as I pronounced it to you, trippingly on the tongue. But if you mouth it, as many of your players do, I had as lief the town crier spoke my lines."

How apt the Bard could foresee the tragic comedy the residents of Hong Kong are so unfortunately subject to.

Mark Peaker, The Peak

Quarantine-free entry for bank CEO slap in face of SMEs

Does Chief Executive Carrie Lam Cheng Yuet-ngor not comprehend that one person does not define the economic interests of Hong Kong? That responsibility has been the burden of the residents of Hong Kong who have, despite the government's draconian and scientifically unproven quarantine restrictions, battled daily to ensure that our economy survives.

That she panders to JPMorgan CEO Jamie Dimon, who was granted a quarantine exception by the government, telling reporters, "After all, it is a huge bank and it has important businesses in Hong Kong", is a slap in the face of every small- and medium-sized business leader, the true leaders of economic development in Hong Kong.

Mark Peaker, The Peak

Procedure for airport arrivals leaves much to be desired

Presently placed in solitary confinement at the behest of Chief Executive Carrie Lam's government as part of Hong Kong's quarantine policy, I was curious as to whether she and the eminently qualified Secretary for Food and Health Sophia Chan, who have the health of the Hong Kong public foremost in their minds, can explain why, after five hours of being processed at Hong Kong airport, there is no social distancing in the last hour as residents and guests to our once great city are herded into queues and then crammed into two lifts before being placed on filthy minibuses with poor ventilation.

Our bus, despite all seven passengers destined for hotels in the Western District of Hong Kong Island, took a much longer route via the Central tunnel. When we asked why we did not take the most direct route, protecting Hongkongers from exposure to us, we were informed that the bus owner only allows them to take the route with the cheapest toll. Apparently, the government outsources airport quarantine transfers to the cheapest operators.

Mark Peaker, The Peak

Patriotism is not a substitute for competence

As this month's Legislative Council elections draw near, the silence from candidates is deafening ("What's a manifesto? Hong Kong Legco candidates' simple slogans, brief statements show 'lack of effort'", December 5). However, the claim by Chief Executive Carrie Lam Cheng Yuet-ngor that a low voter turnout reflects good governance is flabbergasting.

It is absolutely right for Beijing to demand that patriots govern Hong Kong. Patriotism is not, however, a substitute for competence.

The youth of Hong Kong feel disinvested, they feel they cannot effect change. This could be partly because of anti-Beijing sentiment, but also because of frustration and a disdain of a local government they feel ignores them, a distrust seemingly strengthened by a chief executive with an aloof and self-congratulatory manner.

Capability, communication and community are core to the foundation of our city, built upon the skills and dreams of its residents. Hong Kong deserves a local government that also represents the needs of its weakest and poorest as well as its diversity, a government that recognises and nurtures the abundance of talent and guides it towards common prosperity. Good government can, indeed, be silent. What cannot be is results.

Mark Peaker, The Peak

Free rides brought families together

Every Sunday is Shek O day for us, a visit to Lulu's for the best breakfast in Hong Kong and a chance for our dog to enjoy the car trip, ears flapping in the wind. Sunday was notable as the bus terminus, a Grade II historic building with art deco features, was unusually busy with buses disgorging countless families, all eager to vote, sorry, all eagerly enjoying the free use of public transport. Not an entirely meaningless day then, it seems?

Mark Peaker, The Peak

2022

Charity's good work should not be overshadowed

Recent events at the Hong Kong Society for the Protection of Children have cast a pall over a charity that has, for almost a century, worked tirelessly and without fanfare caring for the neediest children of Hong Kong.

Its work remains vital, ensuring that children from homes where family struggles prevent opportunities for development continue to find a safe haven.

The acts of a few shall not undermine the decades of hard work and commitment the staff of the charity have unfailingly given. As a past deputy chair of the charity's fundraising committee, I hope that the generosity of Hong Kong people shall not be dissuaded from continuing support for an organisation which, since 1926, has been a beacon of hope, love and opportunity.

Mark Peaker, former deputy chairman of fundraising, Hong Kong Society for the Protection of Children

Lam in no position to blame Cathay Pacific

It is unacceptable that Chief Executive Carrie Lam Cheng Yuet-ngor chastised Cathay Pacific chairman Patrick Healy and CEO Augustus Tang Kin-wing, summoning them to her office to express her government's "strong dissatisfaction" and stating that there is no excuse for management not to be blamed for the actions of their staff.

She then absolved herself of blame over similar behaviour from her own ministers, stating she would not take responsibility for their personal wrongdoing. This reeks of hypocrisy.

Cathay Pacific has a legacy of service to Hong Kong that goes far beyond this chief executive's tenure. Cathay has for decades served the aspirations and dreams of Hong Kong and its residents. It is wrong to condemn an airline that, despite monumental hardship, has kept families connected and cargo moving throughout the pandemic.

Humiliation is neither warranted nor justified from a chief executive quick to apportion blame to others and slow to accept she, as head of the government, should publicly apologise for the actions of her ministers.

Mark Peaker, The Peak

More than travel sacrificed in quarantine measures

In reducing quarantine for close contacts at Penny's Bay to only 14 days but continuing the requirement that all entries from abroad do a 21-day stay, the government is displaying the same questionable logic as in banning dine-in services at restaurants after 6pm.

Confucius wrote, "If you govern with the power of your virtue, you will be like the North Star. It just stays in its place while all the other stars position themselves around it". Governing by confusion, meanwhile, is creating a meteor shower of panic.

Your correspondent in "We're a Covid-fearing city, live with it" (January 14) misses the point entirely about what is wrong with the government's draconian and unjustified quarantine imposition. He states it is "all good as long as you don't need to travel frequently". Travel is but one element that Hong Kong has sacrificed, along with jobs, families, financial stability, mental health, and the city's status as a centre for international trade and commerce.

The cost is far more than a supposed desire to travel; it is a loss of a right to live *sans* the open prison Hong Kong has effectively become. The world is learning to live with Covid because that is the only viable course to allow people to sustain their lives. Hong Kong must accept this so we can return to the world of normalcy.

Mark Peaker, The Peak

Thank you for the music, Meat Loaf

Since 1977, when I was 14, I have bellowed the music from *Bat Out of Hell* at the top of my lungs on almost any occasion. It was love at first hearing.

That Meat Loaf has passed is sad. Heaven can wait, for the lead singer of a band of angels is wrapped up in our hearts. His songs took us all through lonely nights and through the cold of the day. Meat Loaf came down here just to sing for us and the melody's gonna make him fly, without pain, without fear.

Rest in peace, Meat Loaf.

Mark Peaker, The Peak

To be continued …

Published in 2022 by
Unicorn, an imprint of Unicorn Publishing Group
Charleston Studio
Meadow Business Centre
Lewes BN8 5RW
www.unicornpublishing.org

ISBN 978 1 914414 78 7
10 9 8 7 6 5 4 3 2 1

Design by newtonworks.uk
Printed by Asia One, Hong Kong